*The Author in North Africa, 1943*

# FURTHER MEMORIES OF BIRMINGHAM

By
LESLIE MAYELL

LODENEK PRESS
Padstow, Cornwall

First published 1982

©   LESLIE MAYELL 1982

ISBN O 946143 00 5 Hard Covers
ISBN O 946143 01 3 Paperback

Published by Lodenek Press Ltd., 17 Duke Street, Padstow, Cornwall
Printed by St. George Printing Works Ltd., 1-3-5 Wesley Street, Camborne, Cornwall.

# CONTENTS

# LIST OF PHOTOGRAPHS

Frontispiece: The Author in North Africa, 1943

# ACKNOWLEDGEMENTS

I am again indebted to Mr. John Whybrow of Stratford Road, Sparkbrook, whose photographs of old Birmingham have been a source of pleasure. Many are reproduced in this book.

Two photographs appear by courtesy of the Birmingham Public Libraries Local Studies Department.

Besides permitting me to quote from one of its special editions, the Birmingham Evening Mail has sent me three photographs.

Bass, Mitchells and Butlers Ltd. have not only researched the King's Arms, Alcester Road South, but have presented me with a photograph of the pub.

Last but not least is the large number of people that have written to tell me how much they have enjoyed "The Birmingham I Remember". I have been reminded of many incidents, people, and places I had almost forgotten, but which were brought back to me with vivid clarity. I have woven many of them into the reflections that follow.

Among my correspondents have been many 'boys' and 'girls' who were at Stratford Road School when I was there, yet strangely I have heard from only two who were at Yardley Grammar School in my time.

Sadly I have learnt of the death of quite a number of my old friends, but had I given it thought I should have realised that such was inevitable: most of those still living must now be between 60 and 80.

L.M.

To Lynda

# INTRODUCTION

I drove from my home in Lostwithiel, by-passing Liskeard, to Plymouth, and joined the M5 near Exeter to be in Birmingham when my book, "The Birmingham I Remember," was officially published. On the 24th November 1980 I went to the B.B.C. in Pebble Mill Road to be interviewed "live" by Derek Dingle in his programme, "Good Company."

It was a delightful interview lasting nearly twenty minutes. He had obviously read the book with interest and care......but fancy not knowing what troach and tip-cat were!

The interview ended with an apt song called "Saturday Night in the Bull Ring". It was sung in a gorgeous Brummie accent by Malcolm Stent. Later I obtained the record (disc); on the other side was a monologue by Malcolm called "Sunday Dinner" which made Mary and me hoot with laughter.

But it was not until Peter Ricketts, features' editor of the "Birmingham Evening Mail", had reviewed the book on December 8th that the publishers began to receive orders from Birmingham bookshops.

By the end of January a second printing was being contemplated, and many people had written urging me to write more about the Birmingham I had known before, during, and after the First World War. When a director of Lodenek Press suggested I should start thinking about another book on similar lines, I began to treat the idea seriously. The more I thought about it the more enthusiastic I became, and soon realised that I had enough material for another trip down Memory Lane.

John Whybrow, the photographer who has published those two superb books, "How does your Birmingham grow?" and "How Birmingham Became a Great City", had much to do with my enthusiasm. Apart from allowing me to use many of his magnificent photographs, he had sent a generous letter after reading "The Birmingham I Remember", and two photographs of Stratford Road, Sparkbrook, circa 1905 from his famous collection.

More about those photographs later.

One of the men who wrote to me was a cousin of Mabel Johnson, my first sweetheart. In "The Birmingham I Remember" I told how she and I often walked together from Stratford Road Infants' School to "our entry" in Turner Street from where she continued alone to Highgate Road where she lived.

When I heard from Ted Collins of Wake Green Road, however, I had already met Mabel in a residential home for elderly people in Alvechurch, near

Birmingham. Almost 70 years of age, she was active and high spirited; we immediately recognised each other though more than 60 years had elapsed since we walked home together.

"I've a bone to pick with you," she said when we were comfortable ensconced in her private room at 'The Lawns'.

"Hello!" I thought. "Where did I go wrong?"

"Our shop in Highgate Road was a draper's and not a second-hand clothes shop," she said.

I had to apologise, of course, but added: "Anyhow, that's how it always looked to me from the other side of the road, and I did say in my introduction that I was presenting memory-pictures."

"Well," she replied, pleasantly mollified, "I will admit that it might have given a little boy the impression that it was a second-hand clothes shop."

A long letter came from Jack Atkins of Shirley. I remembered him as a Scout when I was in St. Agatha's Wolf Cubs. He had known my sister Doris and cousin Olive, and said that Olive "was one of the local beauties." Her photograph, taken when she was about 14, appeared in 'The Birmingham I Remember'. She died in August 1980 in Belper, Derbyshire, at the age of 79.

Jack's knowledge of Sparkbrook and its people was considerable, and his first letter was only an instalment of what he was to write.

Two girls — now women — who had remained firm friends since they left Stratford Road Council School more than 50 years ago, wrote to me. One of them told me (half-a-century too late!) that she had a crush on me. She now lives at Llandridnod Wells, Powys, and said my book had filled her with nostalgia.

The other is a widow named Ellen Jones who lives in Hall Green, and it is from her letter that I have learnt something of the more seamy side of the lives of people who lived in Sparkbrook between the wars. Known as Nellie Fisher before her marriage, she worked for 13 years at Holt's, the pawnbroker's near Studley Street in "the Lane", and has given me permission to use the following:

"I suppose I was about four years fully learning the trade and having the ability to value goods and jewellery," she wrote. "The shop was gaslit, but there was no such luxury in the stockrooms upstairs. We used an oil lamp.

"I put goods on display, hanging outside the shop: second-hand suits, jackets, overcoats, and long sticks with nails at intervals on which hung boots and shoes, all unredeemed pledges.

2

"We used to sell rolled-gold wedding rings for about 1/-, a Godsend for the poverty-stricken housewives who pawned their gold ones till the weekend, hoping it would not be missed if replaced with a rolled-gold one.

"It was quite usual to take in pledge an old-fashioned flat-iron still warm with use, for seven old pence which would buy enough stewing beef for a family from one of the many butchers on the Lane. The poverty was something which the present generation would hardly believe.

"I well remember one customer who had got into difficulty and pawned her husband's watch and chain each Monday morning and redeemed it Friday evening after being paid. He wore it only weekends so he did not miss it. However she came to see me one day in great distress because he had asked her to put out his best clothes ready for the evening for a social event at work. She knew he would need the watch and chain; she had not the money to redeem it and said she would commit suicide rather than face him.

"I decided to go straight to my boss, Mr. Holt, who was at the Clifton Road shop to ask his advice. The result was, I took the watch and chain to her house in the afternoon and collected it the following morning on my way to work...."

I must mention the letter I received from Mrs. Jean (Winnie) Gallagher of Olton. I had read in a special issue of the Birmingham Evening Mail that during the blitz of the 19th November 1940 a German bomb on Turner Street, Sparkbrook, had killed one of her sisters. Jean, who was 14 at the time, was badly shaken. I wrote and asked where in Turner Street she had lived. She replied that it was at Harwood's coal-yard — which was only a few yards from where I lived until I married in 1938.

Of course I remembered that large family that moved there as caretakers after Harwoods, having made their pile, went to live in a more salubrious area. Mr. van Asten was one of Harwood's delivery men, and although I could not recall Jean in particular, I remembered that all the children had very fair hair like their Dutch father. But Jean remembered me.

The same newspaper told how "Miss Edith Abel and her sister Laura were having a cup of tea on the cellar steps. In the violent explosion the steps disappeared beneath them and they were swept into the cellar."

Edith and I were in the same form at Yardley Grammar School and she has written to me since reading my book. And she still lives in the same house in St. Paul's Road, Balsall Heath.

This book is a companion to "The Birmingham I Remember" and elaborates, indeed sometimes repeats where I think necessary, what I have already written. It also extends to the outbreak of the Second World War. It is not an autobiography but a book about Birmingham, taking in places I came to know as my knowledge of Birmingham grew.

When I take you into my home in Birmingham, as I do later in the book, it will be like going into most of the homes in Sparkbrook, and indeed in Birmingham before countless council houses and "brick-a-week" semis built by private developers, engulfed Acocks Green, Hall Green, Yardley Wood, Erdington, and the rest of the City's outer suburbs. Therefore with everything I write I am hoping the readers will identify themselves with me.

Again I rely on my wife, Mary, to confirm what I remember and to remind me of what I have omitted, for she, too, grew up in the same locality. Mary Barton was born in Roshven Road, Sparkbrook, in 1913, and went to Yardley Grammar School after attending Dennis Road School until she was 11.

She reminded me, for instance, of the thick dirty yellow fog that sometimes blanketed our winter mornings, and the uncanny quietness that descended on the world as we found our way to school. When we blew our noses our handkerchiefs would be black with the filth we had breathed. On frosty, murky mornings the sun was a big red ball above the roofs and chimney pots of Beechfield Road and beside St. Agatha's massive tower, grey in the mist.

The following could be a footnote to the Introduction of 'The Birmingham I Remember' in which I wrote affectionately of the trams that clanged and clattered along so many of Birmingham's streets and roads (one reviewer wrote: "He dotes on trams,") but I neglected to mention the Illuminated Tram, a point made by more than one of my correspondents.

Yes. I saw it all right. Twice. I think it came out of Kyotts Lake Road depot, and I was taken to see it, probably by Olive, one dark evening in Stratford Road. As it passed I felt the heat of its electric bulbs, otherwise my memory is rather hazy. I know that people crowded the pavement, that the tram was a single-decker, and that it was covered with electric lights of various colours, but mostly yellow.

I don't think the lights formed any particular pattern, and when I said that I had an idea that the letters S.O.S. were to be seen on the front, Mary thought I was confusing it with something else.

But we were both very young and saw it only for a few seconds as it passed...more than 60 years ago!

## MORE ABOUT SPARKBROOK

In the Introduction I mentioned two photographs sent to me by John Whybrow after he had read "The Birmingham I Remember". Had I known they existed I would, with his permission, certainly have included them. They were of Stratford Road, Sparkbrook, and quite the most exciting photographs I had seen. Mr. Whybrow put their date at 1905 when steam-trams were obviously running along Stratford Road because there were rails but no electric cable.

My first reaction was to think how little Stratford Road had changed between 1905 and 1940, but as I examined them more closely my interest mounted.

One shows the Angel when the Eastwoods were there, St. Agatha's Church where I was baptised, and the spire of Stratford Road School which I attended before going to Yardley Grammar School. The trees that darkened our classroom windows can be seen, while on the other side of the road is the large house where Mr. Whybrow now lives. A man is looking at the photographs in the showcase of Thomas Lewis, photographer, which became Lewis and Randall Ltd., in 1919. (It is now John Whybrow Ltd.). Mr. Whybrow has told me that the elm tree, believed to be about 250 years old, was felled in July 1977, after succumbing to the comparatively recent Dutch elm disease. The spire in the distance is that of the Baptist Church on the corner of Palmerston Road which John Whybrow attended years later.

But it is the shop on the corner of Ladypool Road, opposite the Angel, that intrigues me most. It was there I was born, and I was seeing it as a draper's shop for the first time.

I still feel strangely awed when I look at the other photograph. There, in large letters, is the name, THE CENTRAL DRAPERY COMPANY, and below are rolls of material, carpet, and oilcloth my father has put outside. And in the darkness of the doorway stand my father and mother. Perhaps the reproduction does not show them as the actual photograph does, but they are there all the same.

I see other things, too: the street lamp I knew and the stump to which horses were tied while their drivers were in the pub; the horse-drawn milk float, the only traffic on the road; and, on the corner of Long Street, the Victoria Inn which we called the Vic.

While on the subject of photographs, I would like to mention that the one of me with my mother shows that young children wore boots and that trousers did not cover the knees. Boys were 14 or 15 before they went into long trousers, and that was something rather special. As we graduated to them at Yardley the girls in our form looked at us and grinned, and the boys still wearing shorts were jealous and felt undignified.

It was quite usual for those who left school at 14 to start work in shorts, and continue to wear them until they were worn out. The main drawback to shorts, and the one which I remember vividly, was that the inside of the legs above the knees became chapped in winter. Mary says hers did, too. Before I got into bed I would rub Melrose on my chapped legs and found it very effective.

When my mother went shopping up 'the Lane' (Ladypool Road) she bought our potatoes, cabbages, sprouts, and (during the First World War) turnip-tops from Westwood's, a large shop that was open, like a market stall, to both Alfred Street and Ladypool Road. Everything was on a grand scale: the potatoes were heaped high against the back wall and slipped forward as they were sold; the fish, exposed to flies in summer, was on a huge marble slab, and was cut, weighed, and filleted by a fellow who was wet and slimy, and quick and dexterous with a long sharp knife. In Ladypool Road there were great blocks of dates, and the prunes, cherries, blackberries, strawberries, blackcurrants, redcurrants, gooseberries, and raspberries were behind an iron grill to prevent their falling on to the pavement; and behind the assistant were mountains of apples, pears, oranges, lemons, and festoons of grapes, green and black. Bananas were a penny each or four for threepence ha'penny (3½d).

I vividly recall an incident during the First World War. My mother sent my sister Doris, about 11 at the time, to get potatoes at Westwoods. She had been gone such a long time that my mother became worried, and took me with her to see what was happening. In Alfred Street we were confronted by a vast queue of people standing four or five deep, and eventually found Doris, small and white-faced, among them. My mother called her, and when Doris was unable to get out of the surging mass, fetched a policeman to extricate her.

Writing about Highgate Road in 'The Birmingham I Remember', I made no more than a passing reference to the tram depot between Ladypool Road and Stoney Lane, but it was a building that always fascinated me. In addition to its vastness, it had long parallel rows of tunnels over which the trams ran on their rails enabling men to work underneath them. I cannot remember when I did not know this, but I expect I was told, probably by my father, when I was very young.

My Uncle Bill, the husband of another of my mother's sisters who lived in a tiny house against the railway embankment in Henley Street, died of cancer, and I was taken to his funeral. The horse-drawn hearse and coaches slowed down past the depot and a large group of my uncle's workmates, in their overalls, were standing bare-headed and in silence.

I have been reminded that between Stratford Road and Beechfield Road there was a house in Ladypool Road with a board fixed on to the wall, stating that it was where Mr. Deakin, verger of St. Agatha's Church, lived. He is a shadowy figure in a gown of office, but in my mind's eye I see his wife vividly. She was very small, thin, and terribly bent; she always wore black including a large hat, and carried a bunch of keys. To me she was like a witch who had stepped out of Grimms' Fairy Tales, a book I had been given as a Christmas present when I could read, which both fascinated and terrified me.

I have also been reminded that Tommy Hitchman's cab with its horse that seemed to droop at the knees, was often outside the Angel. I remember that it stood in Ladypool Road beside the long whitewashed wall, and was mildly surprised when I first saw it. By 1916, when I started school, such cabs had become rare in Birmingham.

St. Paul's Road was on the right-hand side of 'the Lane', the Balsall Heath side, and ran to Moseley Road. On the corner was a large and rather splendid cake-shop called Wests where my mother sometimes bought cream cheese and pikelets. The cream cheese, unwrapped, of course, like bars of chocolate and most other such edibles, was sold on corrugated cardboard.

St. Paul's Road was regarded as rather 'better' than the other roads round there—at least by its residents! Certainly it was very quiet, and the houses had bay windows and tiny front gardens. A short distance along on the right-hand side was a plaque indicating that Eugene L. Niner gave violin lessons. I was taken there by my mother when I was 9 or 10 and spent two years going to him once a week. I must have been a dreary pupil with no aptitude for the violin, for he seemed to lose interest in me and began using me to run errands. When my mother heard about this she was naturally very indignant, and I was moved to Miss Webster whose house in Stratford Road opposite the school had a lot of steps up to the front door.

Miss Webster struggled with me for two or three years at a guinea for ten lessons. Even to myself I would not admit that I hated it. Actually, the violin was about the worst instrument that could have been chosen for me. My ear for music was appalling and I never knew whether I was sharp or flat. Even today I cannot sing more than half-a-dozen notes without changing key, so I'm told. Yet I love music and have no difficulty in recognising tunes.

On a house nearer to the photographers was a large notice — I think it was of black glass — with one word, BOTTELEY, on it. I discovered that this was where another violin teacher lived, and that was his name. I often saw him in Stratford Road; he was small and wizened, and had an ugly, malevolent face. At least that was how he appeared to me. But probably Mr. Botteley was a very nice man, and I did hear that he was an excellent violin teacher. My correspondent, Jack Atkins, has told me that he and his pals used to call him Dracula. Apparently he wore a black Homberg and full-length black cloak in his younger days, but evidently these had been discarded by the time I was around.

As I have said, many readers of 'The Birmingham I Remember' have written to me, and it has been no surprise that many look back on Birmingham, and particularly on Sparkbrook and 'the Lane', with nostalgia and affection. Possibly it is because so much has changed or disappeared, and that 'the Lane' today with its shops and shoppers is more like a street in Bombay or Calcutta.

Before leaving Sparkbrook I must take another peep into the infants at Stratford Road Council School. Frank Hubball who was born in 1906, lived in 'our building', and was one of my cycling pals, has written to remind me that Mr. Cully, the school caretaker, 'came round the classrooms on dark afternoons to light the gases. These were composed of four burners of a naked fish-tail light suspended from the ceiling on an iron frame.'

I recall this very clearly and how the class went very quiet and the teacher was totally ignored while the children watched Mr. Cully.

Frank told me that he remembered when 'jugs of cocoa and thick pieces of bread were served out to selected children before 8 o'clock in the morning. There was only raspberry jam on the pieces, no butter or margarine.'

Although I don't recall this — perhaps I was never around early enough — I remember that in my first year, the teacher, Miss Turner, who was very tall and whose classroom floor went up in steps, often sent to Pinders, the confectioners on the other side of Ladypool Road, for buns for children who had come to school without breakfast.

1. *Stratford Road, Sparkbrook (looking south)*

2. *Stratford Road, Sparkbrook (looking north)*

3. *The Mermaid, Sparkhill*

4. *Back Houses*

5.   *Nelson's Statue, Bull Ring*

6. *Market Hall, Bull Ring*

7. *King Edward VI High School, New Street*

8. *Exchange Hotel*

# 3

## PEOPLE

Since writing 'The Birmingham I Remember' and receiving readers' letters, I have realised that people and places are closely linked in childhood memories.

'Do you remember the old girl who sang "Count your blessings,"?' wrote one lady who no longer lives in Birmingham but was born in Ladypool Avenue in 1913 and attended Stratford Road Council School.

Of course I remember her, and a lot of other beggars who sang in the horse road in those days.

And did I remember, she went on, the legless ex-soldier who pushed himself along on a home-made trolley, and had a dog with a brass collecting box strapped to his back?

I remember him, too. In every part of Birmingham there must have been ex-service men, many crippled or disfigured, wearing medals of the Great War, who were driven to eke out their miserable pension by begging. The way in which we, as a nation, have treated our soldiers returning from wars does nothing to make us feel proud. It was not until after the last war that our compassion became practical.

In a later chapter I mention how the change from silent films to 'talkies' threw a great many musicians out of work — men for whom music had been their life's work and who could do little else. It was tragic for them, but there was something dignified and rather fine in the way many of them took to the streets and continued to make music,

I recall two such men in the Sparkhill and Balsall Heath districts. One was named Dexter. He had clowned and postured above the orchestral curtain at the Picturedrome on Stratford Road, but played the violin superbly. He was a great showman, and every patron of the Picturedrome must have seen him, transfixed by a spotlight, his eyes closed, and with a huge "diamond" sparkling in a ring he was wearing as he played.

The other called himself Paul Morano. He had been advertised and idolised as the leader of the orchestra at the Alhambra, Moseley Road, but when the job ceased he took to the gutter with his violin; his wife accompanied him to hold out the collecting box for coppers from passers-by.

Everyone who lived in Birmingham during the Great War and its aftermath remembers their particular rag-and-bone man. In Turner Street a thin-faced man wearing a cap and a white muffler pushed his cart, which had thin strips of coloured paper flying in the wind. Every few yards he stopped and blew on a long trumpet. The children of the neighbourhood immediately recognised the sound and asked their mother for pieces of rag. We knew exactly how much rag we needed for a ha'penny.

There was an old lady who came up 'our entry' collecting rags-and-bones. She always wore a man's cap, and would stand at the top of each backyard and shout: "Anything this morning, lady? Anything?"

Mary was born and grew up in Roshven Road which connected Clifton Road with Taunton Road. She has told me that the rag-and-bone merchants sorted their takings in a field where the Carlton Cinema was eventually built. I never saw them doing this, but I remember the incongruous field in Taunton Road.

In the days when there was very little traffic about, many queer contraptions came along the horse road. A horse-drawn cart came round our way. In it there was a piano and a pianist. His name was blazoned on the side of the cart: it was Uno, a man who had lost both his hands in the Great War and played for pennies with the stumps that were left.

Into Turner Street also came a horse-drawn roundabout worked by hand and taking about six children at a time. I climbed on to a horse, paid my penny, and went round and round until I was dizzy. I reeled drunkenly when I got off, and was violently sick in the gutter.

I could tell of many more people: the countless organ-grinders; the knife-grinders who pushed their machines along the road on one large wheel, and when someone gave them knives or scissors to sharpen, turned their machines over, sat on a seat and treadled the big wheel that drove their small whetstone wheel; the ex-soldier who once knocked on our door and asked if he could paint our number — he had a small brush and a little pot of white paint; the man and woman with a cart-load of big blocks of salt who cut off customers' orders with saws; and the various pedlars who came to the back-door with their wares.

I still have the Earl Kitchener memorial card that my mother bought from a man who came selling them at the back-door. I remember quite clearly the incident in 1916 when Kitchener was drowned when the cruiser 'Hampshire' was sunk.

# 4

## OTHER DISTRICTS

When the lease of The Central Drapery Company expired we moved into a house in the same neighbourhood chiefly because my mother had many people 'on the books' of her drapery club. She asked Douglas Gilmore, who owned a large drapers' business on Stratford Road near Kyotts Lake Road, if she could continue for him. He agreed, and she went on collecting sixpences and shillings every week from people who had come to regard her as a friend.

Sometimes she took me on her calls, and I went into back houses and ill-lit slums as well as houses better than ours and roads superior to Turner Street. Sometimes my mother and I went into the homes of men who were in prison, usually for receiving a few shillings from the state without reporting they had done a bit of casual work. Most of them had been in the army and had large families living in abject poverty.

Wherever we went — Sandy Lane, Lawley Street, Bolton Road, Conybere Street, Sherlock Street, Watery Lane, Floodgate Street, and in the back streets of Camp Hill, Small Heath, Balsall Heath, and Digbeth: places which were cold, ill-lit, deserted, and where it was always winter — my mother, a small woman carrying a bag of money and using the same route every week, had no reason to walk in fear of attack 60 years ago.

Jack Eastwood and I were once taken to the Alexander Sports Ground, Aldridge Road, Perry Barr. I don't think it had been opened long. Although I remember very little about the sports, one athlete stands out in my mind. His name was Bluett or Blewitt, and I still see him as a tall, handsome man who won every race he entered, and was the star of the day.

In 1930 my parents bought me my first motor-bicycle, a second-hand James. I knew the youth who sold it; he lived in Aldridge Road in a large house with a lot of steps up to the front door. His name was Ben. It was a Sunday morning. He took me into a near-by cul-de-sac to teach me to drive. Running beside me while I was in first gear, he told me when to change into second.

I suppose I became elated with a new sense of power because I moved into top gear and opened the throttle. The bike leapt forward and in no time I was bearing down on a large gate with I.C.I. painted on it. I had enough sense to close the throttle and brake hard. The bike screamed to a halt inches from the gate. Ben came running up.

"I thought you'd had it," he said, breathless and annoyed. "If the road had been wet you'd have hit the gate and smashed the bike up."

I had learnt my first lesson!

During my motor-cycling days I frequently went to Derby where my cousin Olive, who had married Robert Eastwood from the Angel, lived, and later I took Mary there on the pillion. We crossed from Sparkbrook to Bordesley Green, drove past the Fox and Goose, and then across Hodge Hill Common. I was very interested in the Common when I first saw it, because a pal of mine who lived in Stechford told me that after dark it was infested with courting couples lying around and making love. And I was at an age to listen eagerly to stories of passion and lechery.

We turned down Newport Road to Castle Bromwich and eventually got to Shelton Lock, where Olive lived, via Minworth, Tamworth, and Ashby-de-la-Zouch.

Earlier, when I was a keen cyclist, I must have ridden many times past Lightwoods Park, but it was quite a time before I realised that here, too, were Warley Woods. It was a name I knew well: as a young child I had gone there with my sister Doris on a St. Agatha's Sunday School outing. She must have talked about it afterwards because the name stuck in my mind. I vaguely recall some big trees, but cannot remember woods like those at Shirley or the Lickeys.

However, I do remember the first time I turned at Quinton on to the newly-opened road to Wolverhampton with the cycling club and saw the heaps of rubble and the slums, factories belching out smoke and fire, and, on our right, towns in a vista of smoking chimney stacks that went on and on until they were lost in a permanent pall of smoke. Later a large cinema was built where Wolverhampton Road left the road to Hagley, and soon there was a Roman Catholic church with a huge white cross that seemed to glow in the industrial haze.

A school pal lived in Wharfdale Road, Tyseley, and I often went to his home. It was quite near the school, and from the school gate in Medina Road (where there was a shop we preferred to the school tuckshop) we cycled down one hill and up another, passing a bank with a front garden, and turned off Warwick Road towards Tyseley station. From the bridge over the railway there was an extensive view with St. Agatha's Church tower standing high in the distance and dwarfing the spire of Stratford Road Council School.

The pleasant smell of potato crisps pervaded Wharfdale Road, but I was glad I didn't have to live with it. It was like Bournville. The smell of chocolate and cocoa was pleasant enough, but I wouldn't have wanted it all the time. The smell in Wharfdale Road emanated from Smith's Potato Crisp factory, and I have the impression now that there were potato fields extending to Kings Road which went down to Coventry Road at Hay Mills. I think some of these fields were open to pavements walked every day by hundreds of people going to work at the numerous factories there. One was J.H.Tucker & Co. Ltd. that made electrical switchgear. Another made King Dick motor-cycles.

Doubtless these potato fields have now gone. In our present permissive days such fields would be probably plundered in a single night by an organised band of thieves.

# 5

## BACK IN TOWN

Why didn't I make more of the Bull Ring? is a question I have been asked many times.

But what more could I say? The Bull Ring was the Bull Ring — alive, noisy, colourful, unique: the very "heart and soul of Brum." It no longer exists, at least not as I and past generations knew it. Does it mean that Birmingham no longer has the heart and soul it once had? I wonder! But I am now a stranger, a mere visitor, and must say no more on that score.

There was a statue in the Bull Ring that always intrigued me; it was of Lord Nelson. (See plate No. 5). While still a child I was told that the railings round the statue were marlin spikes from 'Victory', and that the cannon at the corners were also from Nelson's famous ship.

I have read that the statue is still in the redesigned Bull Ring but 'banished to a remote upper terrace.' Frank Hubball has written to say that it is now 'next to a children's roundabout with people sitting around eating fish and chips, meat pies, sausage and chips, hot dogs, hamburgers, etc. out of paper in a sea of waste paper and empty drink tins.'

Like all big cities, Birmingham had many statues, especially in the town centre. One of these, John Priestley, was moved from Victoria Square to Ratcliffe Place in 1913, we are told, but as I was born only two years earlier, it was really before my time. But I do remember seeing Priestley — or was it James Watt? — standing solemnly on a 10-foot pedestal with a yo-yo in his hand.

It was when the students of Birmingham University held their rag and collected money for the hospitals. On that one Saturday in the year arabs and gypsy girls, pirates and senoritas, cavaliers and pierrettes, appeared early in the morning on trams and collected money from passengers. They went into offices and shops in Town rattling tins, simulating high spirits, and feeling very important.

I wonder if they still have a Students' Day in Birmingham!

Incidentally, it was quite normal once upon a time for people to work on Saturday mornings.

Although I mentioned the Market Hall in 'The Birmingham I Remember' I said nothing about Woolworth's just below. I remember the store being built but cannot give it a date. I know it grew rapidly in size and significance, and that no article exceeded sixpence. There was a constantly expanding range of goods, and a girl about to be married could buy from Woolworth's almost everything she would need in the kitchen.

And there was no inflation. Sixpence in 1925 was still worth sixpence in 1935, and healthy competition was making things, if anything, cheaper.

Spiceal Street ran from the bottom of the Bull Ring, with the parish church of St. Martin on the left, to Jamaica Row. It was always a busy street with hawkers selling fruit and vegetables of every description. The wholesale fruit and veg. market was in Jamaica Row, but by the time of day when I went along market business was over and men were sweeping out the rubbish. Shopkeepers like Annie Laight who, with her sister and their aged mother, kept a huckster's shop on the corner of Turner Street and Tillingham Street, often pushed a basket carriage all the way to the market and returned with it loaded, long before I was awake.

On Tuesday and Saturday afternoons the market became Rag Alley. Mary and I frequently went there on a Saturday night. If only I had bought some of the bits and pieces that were being flogged there for a few coppers during the twenties and thirties!

The market stank mightily; so did many of the people who pushed and shoved, and shouted, swore, and haggled.

There were piles of rusty nuts and bolts and divers pieces of ironmongery on the floor; second-hand clothes; oldies and antiques; and deal tables covered with dazzling cheap jewellery, second-hand books, and damaged knick-knacks. There were several crockery stalls, and invariably a crowd where a big, bull-necked vociferous fellow with a hoarse voice, dexterously jangled cups and saucers, plates, dishes, and jerries bedecked with red red roses, occasionally smashing on the floor those he couldn't sell.

And there was the 'professor' who sold pills, potions, and poultices, and had a huge tapeworm in a glass jar.

Rag Alley was quite a place on a Saturday night, I can tell you!

Jamaica Row ran into Cheapside and was crossed by Bromsgrove Street, which was a continuation of Moat Row. Where it joined Bristol Street there were confectioners, tobacconists, pubs, and second-hand bookshops. On the opposite side of Bristol Street was a double pavement with a Roman Catholic church and Bristol Street School. But I didn't go along there often; I seldom had need to do so.

In the same area but farther from the city centre, was St. Luke's Road. It was on a tram route, had a sharp bend, and was cobbled. My father's elder brother was in digs there when he married a young lady living in Summer Hill Road, Spring Hill, with her parents. My Uncle Fred went to live with them.

15

Within four months he had committed suicide by cutting his throat with a razor. It transpired that he had lost all his savings by settling out of court an action for breach of promise of marriage brought against him by an old flame. But that was in 1899, too long ago to be other than a bit of interesting family history.

One of the treats of going to Town with my mother was being taken into the Co-op restaurant in High Street. First we went in a lift to the offices at the top of the building where membership books were handed over a counter for the 'divvi' to be entered.

My mother kept all the little yellow tickets she received from the baker and milkman when she paid them, and from the Co-op where she bought the grocery. At the end of each quarter she totted them up to make sure she was credited with all the 'divvi' due to her.

From the offices we descended to the restaurant in the basement. My mother always had a ham sandwich, bread and butter, and jam; I had a poached egg on toast and a cake. There was a trio that consisted of a man who played the violin, another on the cello, and a lady pianist. We always sat as near to them as we could. It was there that I first heard 'In a Monastery Garden'. I thought it was wonderful.

There were not many restaurants in the centre of Birmingham between the wars. Over Dunn's, the expensive hatters in Corporation Street was Ridgways with large windows through which we could see people eating and drinking. Also in Corporation Street was Patterson's, and next to W.H.Smith's was Yate's Wine Lodge, with a food counter and tall stools. In New Street was one of Joe Lyon's large restaurants with a white-and-gold surround to a window full of cakes. During the middle thirties Mary and I often finished up there after first-house at the Alec, and sat over our Welsh rarebit and coffee just looking at people and occasionally talking to them; as we did one evening to two loquacious young nurses from the General Hospital.

There was also a restaurant in Martineau Street, but I fed there only once. A strong smell of pine disinfectant pervaded the atmosphere; it was a smell I had always associated with lavatories.

I recall a labyrinth of squalid streets off Broad Street before the Hall of Memory was built, but I had no reason to go that way until, in later years, I became a member of the Crescent Theatre. Soon after the Hall of Memory was ceremonially opened, I went to Town to take snapshots of it with the box Brownie Doris had given me. I was thirteen or fourteen at the time.

In Stephenson Place, the Exchange (I think it was an hotel) had an ugly, high clock tower that always reminded me of a witch in her pointed hat. It was conspicuous on the skyline of the City.

Opposite the terracotta, ornate Law Courts in Corporation Street was Central Hall with its tall, square, distinctive, red tower. (I try to use the past tense consistently: these places may or may not still exist).

I went inside Central Hall only twice. The first occasion was to hear speeches by a group of bluestockings (the rear-guard of the Suffragettes, or the vanguard of Women's Lib) urging their large audience to support the people of Spain against General Franco.

The second time was to a concert by the Birmingham Philharmonic Orchestra. First violin was Charlie Preston who had lived at the outdoor just below us in Turner Street, and was an early playmate of mine.

At the bottom of Steelhouse Lane was the General Hospital. In hot weather bedridden patients were put on to a balcony and could be seen from the tops of passing trams.

I went there one Saturday morning. The previous evening I was at Sparkhill Park to play tennis, and while waiting for our turn on the court I opened a tight box of matches to light a cigarette, and it burst into flame. I had immediate attention from a chemist — it was when shops closed at 8 in the evening at the earliest — but next morning I had a huge blister on the palm of my hand. I decided to go to the General Hospital's casualty department. This was a very large ward where doctors, students, and nurses were treating people for all manner of accidents, some rather revolting. A student looked at the blister, called a doctor over, and was told to burst it. He did this, soaked a piece of cotton wool in an enamel bowl of picric acid, slapped it on, and bandaged my hand.

As a young child I was once taken to the Eye Hospital. It was in Easy Row beside those elegant 18th century houses which unhappily have since been demolished. I went there for the removal of a piece of grit: roads were dustier and stonier than they are now.

The Imperial Hotel in Temple Street became known to me when I was about 20. I had discovered 'John O'London's Weekly' in Dr. Haddow's waiting room (which was really part of the hall) in Stratford Road, and decided it was just the paper for me. I joined John O'London's Literary Circle, which met at the Imperial every other Friday.

In a few months I had become one of the chosen to sit at the feet of the chairman, a scholarly man who lived in Middle Park Road, Selly Oak. After the meetings some half-dozen of us would repair to a tiny café in narrow New Meeting Street to drink coffee and to eat wafer biscuits. The café, a Heath Robinson affair, was owned by a pale, good-looking woman who wore a thick plait of hair over her head. We talked knowingly of books and poetry,

17

discussed important issues, and like so many young people at the time, regarded ourselves as the intelligentsia.

In 'The Birmingham I Remember' I mentioned places that played an important role during my formative years, like theatres and the Town Hall, but I was then writing only about my childhood memories. Now, as I move through the thirties to the outbreak of the Second World War, I can discuss them more fully. After all, the war began more than 40 years ago, and that is a long time, even though it seems like yesterday to someone born in 1911.

During the thirties I saw Gerald du Maurier, Leslie Henson, Jack Buchanan, Carl Brisson, Sybil Thorndyke, Gracie Fields, Elsie Randolph, Evelyn Laye, Anna Neagle, all the D'Oyly Carte members, and a host of others who were famous at that time. They all came during the thirties to the Royal or the Prince, and seats were in such demand that we had to queue to book for performances a week or more ahead.

At the Rep in Station Street I saw James Stewart, soon to change his name to Stewart Grainger and become famous, in a Sheridan play, and it was there that I saw many of Bernard Shaw's plays, including ''Back to Methuselah'' which meant going to three shows in one week.

The Town Hall figured largely in my life and the lives of many of my contemporaries. During the thirties I saw and heard Victor Gollancz talking about his Left Book Club; John Strachey on the theory and practice of Socialism and Communism; Jimmy Maxton with his thin face, long hair, and deep hollow voice; dreary Dean Inge; Doctor Barnes, the controversial Bishop of Birmingham; Sir Oswald Mosley in his black shirt; and the tall, white-haired Red Dean of St. Paul's, Doctor Hewlett Johnson. And, of course, there were the lunch-time recitals on the Town Hall's magnificent organ.

When, sometimes, I returned from Town on a 42 tram which turned off Digbeth into Rea Street, left into Bradford Street to grind up the hill past factories into Moseley Road (or was it called Moseley Street at that point?), there was a park on the right that I cannot recall ever entering. Somewhere on my left was Stratford Place, a dirty, dusty and deserted street; from the top of the tram I looked along it with casual interest at Stratford House. Although I could see that it was very old and probably had a history, I never felt the desire to get off the tram and take a closer look at it. I suppose that was because it looked so dilapidated and utterly forgotten.

Nearby was the Dispensary. I know it must have been a large and imposing building but I have to confess that I cannot visualise it. I can, however, recall the interior, or think I can. My mother attended more than 65 years ago and I went along with her because, I suppose, there was no one at home to mind me.

I seem to see a vast waiting room with long rows of forms opposite the doctor's door. When it was a person's turn to go in, everyone moved up a seat. The doctor was always a woman; I expect I only went there on women's days. Or perhaps the Dispensary was for women only.

I remember an occasion when the door opened and I saw my mother coming from behind a screen in her underclothes and wearing large corsets with suspenders dangling from them.

We always finished up at a small counter with a trap-door where the dispenser gave out medicine in large bottles which, at the time, I thought were pop bottles.

# 6

## CINEMAS

I grew up in the Golden Age of the cinema.

Cinemas were called picture-houses or picture-palaces when I was a child and a youth. The word cinema seemed to come later. I still talk of "going to the pictures."

Before the television age, cinemas meant a great deal to us. They were an integral part of life, and I should think that everyone in Birmingham could choose from two or three cinemas within walking distance of his home. I certainly could.

In 'The Birmingham I Remember' I told how I went, or was taken, to the Olympia, Picturedrome, Waldorf, and Moseley Road Picture House, but around 1930 a fresh rash of cinemas appeared.

It was about that time that the Picturedrome in Stratford Road was demolished and a magnificent new cinema, the Piccadilly, built on the site. It was bigger and far finer than its predecessor, and when it first opened seats had to be booked for Saturday evening performances.

The intervals were rather special, even spectacular. The audience watched Harold Stringer, a bespectacled fair-headed man, ascend from somewhere below the stage, seated at the keyboard of an organ. On one occasion Harold Stringer gave us a "treat": after playing the organ he appeared on the stage playing a grand piano, and then played the violin. Perhaps he wanted to show us what an accomplished musician he was. I remembered being told by my future mother-in-law that his salary was £15 a week, which in those days, for an employee, was colossal.

Compton organs were very popular in cinemas. They were like a one-man orchestra. I suppose they added to the large number of musicians the "talkies" had put out-of-work, some literally in the gutter.

About the same time the Imperial on the corner of Moseley Road and Clifton Road was rebuilt, and the Alhambra, also on Moseley Road but nearer Town, had appeared.

The Carlton in Taunton Road became our favourite cinema. On our way there Mary and I would buy half a pound of coconut candy for fourpence (4d) from Hyde's in Ladypool Road, and at the cinema ascended in a small lift to the balcony.

On the subject of the Carlton, on the 25th October 1940 the cinema was hit by a German bomb during the evening performance. I have been told that 'Typhoon', starring Dorothy Lamour, was being shown at the time.

Mr. Jack Matthews of Moseley was on duty as a part-time Civil Defence Worker. In writing about his ordeal, for the Birmingham Evening Mail, he said: 'I entered the cinema via the emergency exit near the screen, and I shall never forget the grisly sight....In the grim light I was confronted by at least three headless corpses in the front seats. They were sitting upright....

'The Home Guard from Dennis Road Drill Hall already had sorted out the dead from the living, and the corpses had been placed in a pile near the box office....'

The lift at the Carlton was not the only gimmick of cinemas erected after the Great War. I went with Jack Eastwood, who lived at the White Swan, Nechells Park Road, to the Delicia soon after it was built in Gosta Green. During the interval a fountain sprang up on each side of the screen, and I recall the cooling, refreshing effect it had on the packed and foetid auditorium.

When 'talkies' were introduced they were not always well received. The first I saw was at the New Imperial and reproduction was so bad that the dialogue was mostly unintelligible. One cinema — I think it was the Carlton — even advertised 'Silent Films Only' as an inducement to patronage. But sound reproduction improved rapidly, and soon all cinemas were equipped for 'talkies'.

During the 1930s Mary and I frequently visited a cinema in Town — depending on what was being shown, of course. My cousin, Olive Marsh, who was 10 years older than I, had often talked about the Scala and the Futurist while I was still going to the penny-rush at the Olympia in "the Lane". She brought the programmes home, and that impressed me. For picture-houses to have printed programmes was unique in my experience, and I was fascinated by the little drawings of the Futurist Fairy and Scala Scribe (or was it the other way round?). When I eventually went into these two cinemas, however, I was extremely disappointed.

Other cinemas came into being in the City centre: the Gaumont in Steelhouse Lane, the West End in Suffolk Street, and various news theatres. For many years I was intensely prejudiced against that part of New Street where the Odeon, together with Littlewoods and office blocks were built after King Edward VI High School had been demolished for commercial profit. Although I mentioned this appalling act of official vandalism in 'The Birmingham I Remember' I was unable at the time to include a photograph of the School, an omission I have now rectified.

Turning again to the Futurist and the 'talkies', I recall travelling along John Bright Street on a tram in May 1929. I remember the date because I was going to Dr. Aldren in Bristol Road for a medical examination. The sun was shining, and as I looked down on to the pavement I saw a long queue of people waiting to go into the cinema. It was the first showing in Birmingham of Al Jolson in 'The Singing Fool', and a small fortune was being made out of records of "Sonny Boy".

# 7
## MYSELF

On the advice of the publisher, I am devoting this chapter to myself. It had been my intention to make this a book about Birmingham and to eschew anything strictly biographical, but the publisher felt that readers might wish to know something about the author, and I am bowing to his superior knowledge.

I think this is the best place to insert such a chapter.

During January 1929 I became a junior clerk at the City of Birmingham Electric Supply Department, and after passing successfully through a period of probation, I was to become a member of the permanent staff provided I was physically fit. That was why I was going to Dr. Aldren in Bristol Road when I saw the queue outside the Futurist.

I shall always remember that examination with some embarrassment. It was a very warm day, and I was unable to pass sufficient urine for a diabetes test. The doctor gave me a glass of water to drink and told me to go for a walk and return to his surgery in half-an-hour's time.

Before working at the Electric Supply Department I was in the accounts office of a firm of electrical switchgear manufacturers where I learned from Mr. Evans, the accountant (who lived in Aubrey Road, Small Heath), how to do copper-plate handwriting for headings in the Kalamazoo loose-leaf sales ledgers. I was always aware, however, that such a job depended upon the vagaries of individuals and the fluctuations of trade. Thus, at the age of 17 my immediate ambition was to enter local government service.

Never mind if the office was on the top floor of a very old building in Albert Street, that it had tiny Victorian factory windows that were never cleaned, and that it required lights all day, I was a member of the Municipal Officers' Guild, and that was a great step forward!

It was a technical department, and most of the men in that long frowzy room into which the sun never penetrated, were qualified engineers — the sort who wore bowler hats and spats, plus-fours on Saturdays, had cars, and never got their hands dirty. Most of them were in their thirties and had taken part in the Great War. Their experiences were still vivid. They were a high-spirited bunch, and I roared with laughter at their war stories and smutty jokes told in uninhibited language.

I wonder if any of them are still alive! I doubt it. But they remain clear, vital personalities in my memory: Ted Hansom who went through the motions with his golf clubs every Saturday morning in the office, Monty Stevens known throughout the electric supply department as Stevo, Bob Cull, Arthur Wolverson, Ryan Bell, and Arthur Cox who lived at Kings Heath and was so very proud of his twin sons, both of whom were killed 12 years later flying in the R.A.F.

My immediate boss was George Field. He had been in the Royal Field Artillery and ridden a horse. From him I heard many hair-raising accounts of his experiences in the Ypres salient. He lived in Flaxley Road, Stechford.

The clerical head of my department whose office was in the adjoining Dale End building, was a very tall man named Jim Hemming. He was a fascinating person, and had been a sergeant-major on the Italian front. When the Second World War was imminent and the authorities were tightening up, he was arrested for possessing an Austrian revolver. It was an absurd charge preferred by the police who obviously had been alerted by someone with a grudge against him. But questions had been asked in Parliament so the police had to take action.

We all knew about this revolver; it was brought as a war souvenir from Italy; it was a source of laughter and leg-pull. I was chosen to go to the Law Courts in Corporation Street as a witness to Mr. Hemmings excellent character and great patriotism. The case came before the stipendiary magistrate, Lord Ilkeston, but I was never called to the witness box: the police withdrew the charge, confiscated the revolver, and Jim came out of the courtroom unblemished. Within a few days he was his normal high-spirited self.

By 1936 the Electric Supply Department had grown considerably, and I was moved into the position previously occupied by George Field. We had gone to the top floor of an old warehouse on the opposite side of Albert Street. Four young fellows were under me.

The five of us sat at a long table under the windows; we made eyes at the sales girls in The Beehive opposite, slung apple-cores, rubbers, and paper-clips at one another, but did a great deal of work of which a record was kept.

One of the boys came from Ludlow and had matriculated at the grammar school there. He was 6-foot tall, handsome and slender, and had a delightful personality. When he came to Birmingham and joined us he was a devout Christadelphian like the rest of his family, and told us that he would go to prison rather then become a soldier. We argued against him incessantly, and after a few months he became more agnostic than any of us.

His name was Charles Pierce, but we of course called him Tom. He became tremendously interested in speech-training and the theatre, and won a gold medal in a very short time. He grew his hair long, wrote poetry, and was given small parts at the Alexandra Theatre. I believe he had a great future, but the war ended his hopes and dreams. On reaching 20 he was conscripted into

*9.   Suffolk Street Technical College*

10.  *Hall of Memory*

11. *Stratford House*

12. *Carlton Cinema after bombing, 1940*

13.   *Grandmother Yardley (née Louisa Maria Thorp) with Doris. Taken in 1906*

14.   *The King's Arms (The Nob), Alcester Lane South, Kings Heath*

15.   *Digbeth Institute*

*16. Earlswood*

*17. The Swan, Yardley*

the R.A.F. and sent to the Far East. The last known of him was that he had organised and taken part in concerts, and thrown himself whole-heartedly into maintaining the morale of other British troops in Japanese prisoner-of-war camps. I can well believe this: he was ebullient and dynamic. He died or was killed somewhere in Burma.

Poor Tom Pierce! Perhaps he would still be alive, and famous, had I not helped to turn him against Christadelphianism. No one will ever know what hardships, cruelty, disease, and degradation this sensitive boy from Ludlow Town suffered at the hands of the Japs.

Just before war broke out the Department insisted that we should all be experienced in handling stirrup pumps and how to deal with incendiary bombs. Also a long, thick rope was fixed on the ceiling of our room; in the event of our being cut off from the wooden staircase by fire, we were to put the rope through the window and slide down it into the street below.

This rope, and the tall ladder beside it, immediately became magnets not only for the men who worked in Albert Street, but for those in the General Office in Dale End, the Mains Department upstairs, and the Commercial Department downstairs. They came to try their strength and skill by shinning up the rope to the high ceiling or going hand-over-hand up the ladder.

Men in the employ of the City of Birmingham were not allowed to volunteer for the forces other than by special permission, but had to wait until their call-up. After Dunkirk, however, there were so many gaps in the British ranks that men up to the age of 30 could volunteer for certain corps. I did this and went to barracks in Thorp Street, off Hurst Street, to be medically examined and to swear an oath of allegiance to King George, his heirs and successors.

After my initial infantry training I was sent, with many others, to slap yellow paint over European camouflage on vehicles of war which were now destined for North Africa.

More than 5 years were to pass before I returned from North Africa and Italy to Dover. By that time I was the sergeant-major of my unit. I remember ringing the bell of my flat in Clarence Road, Handsworth, fairly late on the last night of 1945.

During the final months of my army years I had heard about the acute shortage of school teachers in the U.K., and many of my friends and relatives had written suggesting I should give thought to it. During my demobilisation leave I applied for college training, was interviewed, and accepted. I have often thought I might have been better off had I continued in local government. Certainly I should have had more free time to concentrate on things that really mattered to me.

Going back in time to the early thirties, I suppose I was about 22 when I became for the first time (and the last) a bearer at a funeral. Mary worked at the Britannic Assurance Company with a girl named Mirrie. She lived with her family in St. Benedict's Road, Small Heath, and was 21 when she was found to have consumption. She went to Romsley Sanatorium near the Clent Hills for several months, but was eventually sent home. As the disease took toll she became thinner and weaker, and we ceased visiting her when she became too weak to move from her bed. When she died her parents, religious and family-loving, were broken-hearted.

She had not been dead more than a few months when her brother of 20, tall and smart and a salesman in a high class City emporium, succumbed to the disease. Christian Kunzle, the cake and chocolate magnate, arranged for him to be flown to Kunzle's T.B. sanatorium at Davos, Switzerland, but it was no use. In a matter of weeks his parents went to Switzerland to bring him home to die. I was asked by his father if I would be one of Laurie's bearers.

That was how consumption struck in those days!

If I have given the impression that unemployment, disease, rumour and preparation of war, and a universal shortage of money made life in the 20s and 30s dreary, solemn, and unhappy I cannot have told the whole story. Like countless others, I look back and see the period as an uncomplicated time, full of promise, laughter, and adventure, and far more colourful than it is today.

# 8

## DANCE HALLS

In 'The Birmingham I Remember', I spoke of dancing which for me began at the age of 13. It was really an awakening interest in girls rather than the actual dancing that attracted me. My first awareness was while I attended Stratford Road Old Scholars Club. Later came the Saturday evening dances at Dennis Road School, where I met Mary Barton.

I went to many such 'hops', we called them, in the late twenties, but during the thirties I became more choosy and, I suppose, better off financially. As I mentioned in my previous book, Moseley and Balsall Heath Institute remained a favourite of ours, but we also went to Tony's Ballroom in Hurst Street, the West End in Suffolk Street, and that most splendid and enjoyable of all ballrooms, the Palais de Danse in Monument Lane.

For many years the Palais had been synonymous with ballroom dancing in Birmingham. When I first went there I was dismayed by its cheap, mean exterior, but what a contrast awaited me inside! That first visit was, I think, to a dance arranged by the Junior Imps (the Junior Imperial League), and the distinguished guest was monocled Sir Austen Chamberlain. He made a political speech, of course, and I was struck by his voice which was harsh, strident and, I thought, rather coarse and hardly in keeping with his monocle and white tie and tails. I had seen pictures of him many times, but not close-ups and side-faced as I saw him now. His long aggressive chin surprised me.

Above all, Mary and I liked going to all-ticket dances held by firms or charitable organisations at the Botanical Gardens, Edgbaston. Having put our coats in the cloakroom we walked past big, wild-eyed, colourful cockatoos that screeched at us from the perches to which they were chained, and through glass-houses where the atmosphere was heavy with humid heat and the scent of lush tropical trees, flowers, and creepers. We always stopped to look at the crocodile (or was it an alligator?) which lay in a comatose state half in and half out of the water. Then came the refreshment bar and finally the ballroom.

It became a ritual for us to go to the Masque on Christmas Eve. It was a delightful, luxurious little dance-hall we had watched being built in Walford Road off Stratford Road. The Old Yardlians occasionally held dances there. Although we usually patronised them, I met only two who were in my form years earlier: George Hughes, the boy who had lived in Wharfdale Road, and Ethel Hebblethwaite whose father kept a butcher's shop somewhere on the south side of the City.

27

Mary and I were married in 1938 at Edmund Street Register Office, and went to Blankenberg in Belgium for our honeymoon. In the back streets of the town we discovered a dance-hall patronised by the local Flemings. Most of the young men were fishermen or agricultural workers; the girls were fair-haired, poker-faced, and danced with a heavy, flat-footed tread. By the end of the fortnight we were going there every evening and were sorry when the time came to leave.

The dance-hall seemed full of flashing lights of different colours, and claimed to have the biggest organ in the world. We didn't know about that, of course. It was a Compton type, but was never played too loudly.

On the rare occasions we go to dances now, we find ourselves longing for the dance music of 50 years ago and how it was played. Today it seems that all music has to be amplified, and dancers have to endure the painful, ear-splitting effect of electric guitars, drums, shrill 'organs' played with one hand, and screaming singers of groups who consider the dancers' requirements as of minor importance compared with their own image.

# 9

## MUSIC

My father and his family were musical, but my mother was tone-deaf. Unfortunately my sister, Doris, and I inherited the musical inability of our maternal side.

As she went about her household chores, my mother sang hymns softly and quite tunelessly, and in my earliest recollection Grandmother Yardley sang 'Come to the Rooshun war, boys, come to the Rooshun war' over and over again without the slightest vestige of melody in her voice.

I accepted her singing as a small child does accept such things, but when I became an adult I realised that she, too, had been tone-deaf, and had not the slightest idea where Russia was or even that such a place existed. She must have been about 20 years old at the time of the Crimean War, and at 80 still sang the songs popular when she was young.

She also sang 'Up in Abloon', and not until many years later did I realise she meant 'Up in a Balloon'. I cannot recall her singing more than these two first lines, and as she was unable to read — a fact she was proud of because she "never had the time to bother" — I doubt if she knew what she was singing about.

My father had a phonograph before the Great War. The wax cylinders were kept in the sideboard in the front room. Each was in a round box lined with wadding and bearing a picture of Edison. The machine had a thin steel rod with a chain attached to support the trumpet, and a soft brush was kept in the living room to remove dust from the permanent needle.

I remember 'White Wings' and 'Silver Threads Amongst the Gold' but my favourites were 'The Death of Nelson' because the boom of cannon could be heard, and 'I'm afraid to go home in the dark' with its background of weird, blood-curdling noises, the howling of cats and their strangely human moaning at night.

Snatches of others come to me after more than 60 years. There was one that went 'I'm looking for a sweetheart and I think you'll do'. (These were the days when 'chauvinistic piggery' was accepted without question by adoring males and normal, truly feminine girls who loved being idolised and wooed). Two others began 'Tax the bachelors, tax them every one', and 'Twenty young coppers were on the corner of the street'.

My father must have been partial to a comic singer named Billie Williams: there were several of his cylinders but I only remember his name.

During the Armistice celebrations of 1918 I took the phonograph into the street and stood it on a chair. With all the noise going on it could not be heard, and Mrs. Lines, who lived lower down, opened her front door wide and put a record on her 'modern' gramophone which had a large trumpet. People listened for a moment or two then started laughing and shouting and screaming again, and drowned the music.

Cousin Olive could play the piano, so could her friend Dolly Morgan who lived in Durham Road off Stoney Lane. I suppose I grew up, like the majority of others, in a very ordinary musical atmosphere. Olive and Dolly played ballads which Bob Eastwood and his friends sang formally. They were such songs as 'That Old-fashioned Mother of Mine', 'Devon Boys', and 'Just a Song at Twilight'.

When Dad came home from the war he got rid of the phonograph and we had a gramophone with a horn and a little tin box of needles that were used for only one record each. He bought records of military bands playing marches and the music of the Gilbert and Sullivan operas. Incidentally, he, too, could play the piano, mainly hymns from memory. I don't think he ever had lessons or could read music.

Poor old Dad! He was a gentle, lovable man whose story must be that of many Midlanders of his generation. He joined Kitchener's Army and wore an arm-band until he was called up, a draper's manager aged 42, in 1917. He went first into the Worcestershire Regiment and was later transferred to the 5th Devons, probably because that regiment had suffered heavy casualties and needed to be made up.

More than 20 years later I went into the army and remember thinking how he must have suffered at the hands of young lance-jacks and corporals. I was still in my twenties, but recall as if it were only yesterday the agonising months that passed before I became reconciled to army life. I hardly dare think about how he must have felt at his age with a wife and three children at home.

After a short infantry training he went to France. The snow and rain, and the mud-filled trenches of that dreadful winter of 1917-18 caused a condition that remained with him for the rest of his life. He returned to England on a stretcher with Bright's Disease and was in a military hospital for several months.

Returning to civilian life, he found that drapery was no longer considered a trade, and that women shop assistants were being employed at low wages; there was no longer work for him. He took various jobs in warehouses in the City, and with unemployment rising, worked for a time in a suburban factory; it was not until 1928 that he was able to return to drapery.

But his complaint was getting worse, and from the age of 60 he gradually deteriorated physically and mentally. He eventually sank into a coma; the reason for death was given as 'Uraemia and chronic interstitial (sic) nephritis'.

But to return to music...

Mary has told me that she remembers how her mother, who was 12 years younger than mine, sang as she did her housework, and the woman next door joined in. Those were the days before radios, spin driers, vacuum cleaners, and other labour-saving gadgets which do not encourage singing about the house.

The woman who was to become my mother-in-law had a strong voice and an excellent sense of pitch which her children have inherited. The songs she sang as she worked in her home in Roshven Road were songs of the Great War — 'Keep the Home Fires Burning', 'Roses of Picardy', 'There's a Long Long Trail a'Winding', 'Let the Great Big World Keep Turning', and songs from musical comedies of the time which have been made known to subsequent generations by T.V. 'Music Hall' programmes such as 'Those Were The Days'.

By the mid-twenties I was having some influence on the records my father bought. 'Bye-bye Blackbird' and 'Shepherd of the Hills' were two of my favourites, and it was during this period that we had a new gramophone: a large cabinet with a space for records and a little door at the front to let the sound out.

In the early thirties my interest in dancing and dance bands, together with my financial ability to buy the records I wanted, resulted in a rapid increase in our collection. Today I deeply regret giving away all my 78s. Each one had some special significance. Some of those numbers are occasionally broadcast today such as 'Happy Days and Lonely Nights', 'If I Had You', and 'You Were Meant for Me'. There were others I remember with the same pleasure — 'Just Half-way to Heaven', 'I'll Always be in Love with You', 'Just a Little Fond Affection', and so on.

Needless to say I never missed those delightful American musicals like 'Broadway Melody', 'Sunny Side Up', 'King of Jazz', and 'Marianne'. And I thought Janet Gaynor and Charlie Farrell were superb.

There is, I know, no going back, but I am glad I grew up in the sentimental and romantic days of the twenties and thirties, when we danced through a sentimental and romantic adolescence with no thought of skinheads and knifings and dance hall brawls.

We always knew when the last dance came, even when it was not announced. The lights went low, and the band played softly and plaintively the last waltz. Inevitably it was one of three melodies: 'I'll See You in my

31

Dreams', 'Who's Taking You Home Tonight', or 'Goodnight, Sweetheart'. Here and there it would be marked by a rapid change of partners, almost everyone would be on their feet, and a romantic hush would fall upon the dancers as they embraced their partners more closely....and then they would walk home in safety.

On the book list my parents received when I started at Yardley Grammar School in 1923 was a song book, and during the next year or two we learned many of the songs from Miss Rose. I still know the words and tunes of 'My Love's an Arbutus', 'Pretty Polly Oliver', 'Fair Are the Flowers in the Valley', 'Tom Bowling', 'Richmond Hill', and many others.

We were creating a bit of school history (without knowing it) when, after assembly each Friday morning, we sat on the floor of the hall and listened to the gramophone, wound up after every record by our be-gowned headmaster, Ponty Lunn. Then he would start us off by singing quite suddenly the first verse of the sea shanty 'Billy Boy' or 'What Shall We Do with a Drunken Sailor?'.

He made the first forms scramble to their feet, face the rest of the school, and sing 'Shenandoah'; and when we sang 'Green Grow the Rushes-ho!' every form had its own part to sing. On special occasions we sang 'Forty Years On' which had been chosen as our school song.

But those were school songs to be kept in a separate pigeon-hole. I suppose it was not until well into the thirties that I began to see music all of a piece, and that there were no arbitrary lines separating the 'good' from the 'bad', folk music from dance music, and so on.

I think it began with seeing 'Bitter Sweet' at the Theatre Royal in New Street, for I had no preconceived category for Noel Cowards music. I shall never forget the effect both the story and music of 'Bitter Sweet' had upon me. I was at the age when one can feel agony and ecstasy. Ever since that time I have been haunted by 'I'll See You Again', and I think my wife has too.

(In one of his plays Noel Coward said: "Strange how potent cheap music can be!").

We became utterly devoted to Noel Coward. I bought all his records and we kept a scrap book of pictures and newspaper cuttings, but it did not survive the war we plainly saw approaching.

Up to the outbreak of the Second World War in 1939 the songs of the streets, of the dance bands, and of the popular radio were what Mary and I liked best, and we kept well abreast of such music. Probably the last two songs that caught our imagination were the Ink Spots singing 'Maybe' and 'Whispering Grass'. I mention these two because the A.T.S. girls at Chilwell,

32

Nottinghamshire, where I did the first part of my infantry training, insisted on that record whenever they were in the Cosy Cafe, just outside the depot, and it was played over and over again.

## 10

## ERASMUS ROAD TO DIGBETH INSTITUTE

I became eligible to join Stratford Road Old Scholars Club at the age of 12, and it was there, a few years later, that I met Hilda. She lived with her widowed mother, a spinster aunt, and an elder brother who had been born in 1910. Hilda was a tall slim girl, good-looking and with an attractive, vivacious personality.

Erasmus Road was the second on the right after Stratford Road, going towards Sparkbrook, had passed under the railway bridge at Camp Hill. Vivian Bird, author and journalist, tells us in his 'Portrait of Birmingham', that it was named after Erasmus Darwin, the 18th century scientist and grandfather of the famous Charles who wrote "Origin of Species".

It was through Hilda that I first came to know her brother, Arthur Hughes. He and I had a great deal in common, and soon we were spending one evening a week together when we talked literature, put the world right, and played table tennis.

Soon the Hughes family moved from Erasmus Road to Appian Close, Kings Heath. Hilda attended the Friends' Institute, Moseley Road, and was a Sunday School teacher there. Miss Dorothy Cadbury built Appian Close, a cul-de-sac off Alcester Lane South containing about 60 small houses, for families associated with the Friends' Institute. Mrs. Hughes must have made an application and obtained one.

I spent many evenings there, and later, when George VI was crowned, Mary and I were invited to join in the jollification arranged for the people living there. It rained heavily in the afternoon, but a large marquee had been erected on a grassy patch at the end of the Close for the children's tea-party. Afterwards Charlie Chaplin films were shown by a man named Alfred Hook who, before moving to Appian Close, lived at Woodbine Cottage which was next to Harwood's coalyard in Turner Street.

Unexpected things happen when a book has been written. Last June I received a letter from Mrs. Winifred Walker of Lancing, Sussex, who had read 'The Birmingham I Remember'. She told me that she had once lived in Turner Street and that Alfred Hook was her uncle. As a child she often visited Woodbine Cottage. Above all she remembered her Aunt Lucy who died at the age of 70.

I, too, remember Lucy Hook. She was a tiny young lady who was one of Olive's friends. Mrs. Walker sent me a photostat of a page in Lucy's autograph album on which Olive had written in 1920. I have sent it to Olive's elder daughter, Jean, who was born in Turner Street, and now lives at Duffield, Derbyshire. Jean is a woman of 56.

After Erasmus Road came Priestley Road, so-named because John Priestley had resided there: once there was a plaque on the wall announcing the fact. Then came Main Street where Mary lived until she and I were married. She was staying there when the house was hit during that terrible German air-raid in November 1940. Fortunately she, her mother, and other members of the family were in the Anderson Shelter in the garden, but that night number 92 ceased to exist.

While I was attending Yardley Grammar School, Tyseley, Arthur Hughes was being educated at the School of Art, Moseley Road, opposite Moseley and Balsall Heath Baths. The school was on the corner of Lime Grove, a tree-lined cul-de-sac at the end of which a narrow path ran by the side of the railway line to Clifton Road. These paths were dark and secluded, and popular with courting couples. I knew only the one from Lime Grove to Clifton Road, but my wife tells me there were several beside the railway. I wonder how she knows!

On Sunday afternoons Arthur and I met at Digbeth Institute. Its denomination was Congregationalist, and he had introduced me to the men's P.S.A. (Pleasant Sunday Afternoon). We were by far its youngest members, and I blush now to think how we held forth on world-shattering events and important problems, while our elders, many grey and old with all the knowledge of years, listened to us, nodded and smiled and smoked their pipes.

The minister, Mr. Bevan, was a plump, handsome Welshman with a fine head of auburn hair. He always wore a morning suit, wing-collar, and spats, and sat with his legs on a chair because he had phlebitis. He had an excellent manner and was knowledgeable on all things — or seemed to be. He, too, always listened to Arthur and me with grave good-humour and courtesy.

When I stayed at Appian Close in summer, Arthur and I occasionally played tennis on courts near a greyhound racing track. It was a fairly new pastime in Birmingham, and from the crowds we saw there it appeared to have caught on.

On the other side of the road, at the tram terminus, was a popular pub affectionately called The Nob. Its real name was the King's Arms. People went there from far and near on Sunday evenings. I suppose some went as far as they could by tram with the intention of having a country stroll (for that was where the country started, on the road to Alcester, in those days), but called in to have one and got no farther.

In his letter to me the present licensee said: 'I have collected off old customers such things as its nickname ('The Nob'). It came, so I am told, from the rich people of Moseley driving out in their carriages with their families for a Sunday evening drive. Their children played on the lawns which were on the side of the pub in those days.'

The Public Relations Officer of Bass, Mitchells and Butlers Ltd. has kindly made available a photograph of the pub. The building was modernised in 1939; the photograph (No.14) was taken in 1964.

It was in the thirties that I went to Hilda Hughes' marriage at Digbeth Institute. The ceremony was conducted by Mr. Bevan. The bridegroom was a handsome young man from Wales who was a constable in the Birmingham Police Force. I believe he 'lived in' at Digbeth Police Station. It was a white building where the road began to climb up to the Bull Ring. It had an absurd clock tower and looked out of place among the smoke-blackened brick buildings of Digbeth.

## 11

## PLACES BRUMMIES VISITED

All Birmingham people went to the Lickey Hills sometime in their lives. Many went frequently, especially if they lived at Northfield, Longbridge, Rubery, Rednal, Barnt Green, or anywhere else in that area.

In 'The Birmingham I Remember' I described the Lickeys as a miniature mountain range complete with woodland, conifer forest, streams, and waterfalls; and there had been tea-rooms, fun fairs, and golf links there as long as I could remember. Though much of it showed the hand of man, it was nonetheless beautiful. What better playground could the people of a big city ask for? I understood that it was maintained by the City Fathers for Birmingham citizens, and they certainly made the most of it.

In my previous book I told of my early visits to the Lickeys and how I was taken to Camp Hill station — which was in Highgate Road and nowhere near Camp Hill — from where the train went to Barnt Green. We walked through Cofton Woods to Bilberry Hill.

In later years Mary and I often visited the Lickeys, but etched on my mind is going there on our motorbike one Sunday afternoon in September 1939.

During the morning I had listened to the Prime Minister, Neville Chamberlain, telling the nation over the radio that from 11 o'clock that morning we were at war with Germany. I was having a bath at the time and listened with the door open as I luxuriated in hot soapy water. We had been married little more than a year and were in our first home, a flat over a shop in Warwick Road, just past Knights Road, in Tyseley.

We were silent and thoughtful during lunch. The Great War with its horror and four years of attrition was relatively fresh in our memories. Our families and the people we knew still talked about it. Mary's father who had been killed at Ypres in 1917, would have been under 50 had he been living, and the country still had a great many war widows and bereaved mothers.

We felt we needed to get away from it all, which was why we went to the Lickey Hills, on that day strangely deserted for a mellow Sunday afternoon.

As we looked down on the Austin works with many of its buildings already camouflaged with green, brown, and black patches, we listened for the drone of enemy planes. Later, as we passed through the long period of "the phoney war", it seemed so absurd, but on that first day we just didn't know what to expect.

I have a very clear recollection of being taken for a day at Earlswood Lakes. It must have been in 1919, for I was with my mother and father, and he was in civvies. Perhaps my sister Doris was with us, but I don't recall her presence.

As we walked to Small Heath station in Golden Hillock Road the weather was excellent. It held while we were on the train to Earlswood, but no sooner were we there than rain started. It became torrential. I don't think I saw the lakes. My father had not brought his raincoat, and his navy serge jacket shone with water, and water ran from his new trilby.

While we were sheltering under the trees with other day-trippers, a flat, horse-drawn cart like those used for delivering coal, rumbled past. It was full of German prisoners wearing the peakless caps that had become so familiar in newspaper pictures and cartoons. One of the Germans dropped a cigarette, got off the cart, retrieved his fag, and with a little run jumped on the cart again in a sitting position. The people sheltering booed and hissed, but the Germans appeared not to notice. Nor did the two Tommies sitting at the front, one holding the reins.

Perhaps it was during that same summer that my parents took me to Sutton Park. We went as far as we could by tram then walked. We watched men riding horses, but of the park itself I remember nothing. I believe I swam in one of the pools in later years, but the park seems to have made no impression on me. I mention it only because I know that it attracted many Birmingham people who regarded Sutton Park as somewhere special. Mary says she was often taken there when a child.

I got to know Sutton Coldfield during my cycling days. I often cycled through Town, up Gravelly Hill to Sutton Coldfield, from there to Lichfield, Burton-on-Trent with its many level-crossings and smell of beer, and on to Derby where Olive lived. Being flat it was good cycling country, but the road was singularly devoid of scenery.

As a keen cyclist I went to the annual Cyclists' Memorial Service at Meriden, where a white monument shared the village green with an ancient cross reputed, like a tree near Leamington, to be the centre of England. Meriden was on the road to Coventry, and we felt we were in the country as soon as we had passed the Swan at Yardley. I don't know whether the annual service is still held, but in the twenties the village green was full of cyclists attending it, including men with wives or girl friends on tandems. Some had come long distances.

After leaving Meriden the road presented a stiff climb over cobbles, an unusual feature in the country. Nearby a lane went off to the right. There was a large crucifix on the corner; it was probably a war memorial. The lane went to Berkswell, a small village with a well where people filled their jugs and buckets. Nearby was the church which had a crypt.

38

This was a popular evening run of ours; Berkswell was a delightful spot, and we liked the ride home through narrow lanes by way of Temple Balsall to Warwick Road. It was not until years later, when looking through the Census Returns for 1871, that I discovered that my paternal grandmother, Mary Anne Richards, was born there in 1840. Later she had kept a milliner's shop in Wednesbury, where she died in 1880.

When I was nine or ten Jack Eastwood and I spent a month at Shenstone, a village off the main road to Lichfield, and about three miles from that city. We were taken there by train, the longest rail journey I could remember, at that time, though I had been told that when very young I was taken to Doveridge in Derbyshire where an aunt kept the village post office.

At Shenstone Jack and I stayed at a pub called the Plough and Harrow, kept by a Mr. and Mrs. Warner. They had an ebullient 16-year old daughter who played the piano and sang irrepressibly. Sufficient to say that when we weren't playing with the local kids or climbing trees, we were watching the blacksmith, a man named Harrison (which seemed to be the name of half the villagers!) in his smithy a few yards from the Plough and Harrow. He was a thin, dour man who swore at horses if they moved while he was shoeing them. When I think of that holiday I smell the peculiar acrid odour of the thick smoke of burning hooves as the blacksmith tried the shoes for size.

In 'The Birmingham I Remember' I did not mention Calthorpe Park, on the corner of Edward Road and Pershore Road, for two reasons. First because I had always regarded it as a bit of a mud patch and not to be compared with nearby Cannon Hill Park; second because I had never been through its gates while still a child.

When war broke out in 1939 there was a display in Calthorpe Park by the City Fire Brigade, and I was invited to attend. King George VI and Queen Elizabeth came. The King was in R.A.F. uniform; so was the Earl of Dudley who accompanied them. A friend of mine took a photograph as they passed close to us, and I still have it. (Plate 19) I was struck by the loveliness of the Queen's complexion and the colour of her eyes, and had to admit that none of the photographs I had seen of her did her justice.

## 12

## GAMES

Many of the people writing to me have mentioned the games they played during their childhood in the first two or three decades of this century. This was not surprising. With the legions of children in the streets from morning till dark, and often after, games had an important place in life.

These were not continued in the somewhat artificial community of the school playground: there was no time before school and playtimes were too short for us to get really organised. Nor were our school friends the same as those of our streets. At school we tended to gravitate towards boys in our particular class — or standard, as we called them at Stratford Road. With two or three other boys I should have been in the top standard for three years had we not been sent to grammar schools. Those were the days when classes were composed of children of similar scholastic achievement, and such extraneous characteristics as emotional development were not considered as they are today now that the 'trick cyclists' have, unfortunately, taken over.

Streets, between the wars, were more alive than they are today with impersonal motor-cars and lorries hurtling around. People walked or cycled home to dinner, then went back to work, and women and old men stood on their front steps and gossiped with their neighbours. There was an old woman living opposite us in Turner Street who stood for hours at the bottom of Salford Place; when the sun became too hot or glaring she crossed over and sat on our doorstep because our side of the street was always in the shade.

In 'The Birmingham I Remember' I mentioned tip-cat and various other games we played in the horse road. While we were playing boys' games the girls frequently had a skipping rope across the road from one footpath (pavement) to the other; girls ran in, skipped, then ran out again while the rope was still turning.

There were little songs too, and they come back to me over the years with surprising clarity. As they turned the rope the girls would sing:
"Early in the morning at six o'clock
You may hear the postman knock.
'Postman, postman, drop your letter.
Lady, lady, pick it up.' "

The girl skipping would carry out the actions with her handkerchief — or more likely the bit of rag that served as a handkerchief — while she skipped. Girls in our district became extremely proficient at skipping.

Another of their games was for a girl to skip in front of her friends and sing:

> "House to let apply within,
> I call Mary Barton in...."

at which the girl named would run into the twirling rope, and skip facing her friend, but gradually turning round until both girls were facing the same way. Then the first girl sang:

> "House to let apply without,
> I send Mary Barton out."

And out would run the girl.

Mary told me that when she first played she had no idea what the words meant, and for quite a long time sang: "House to letta ply within...."

She had reminded me that often when we played Hide-and-Seek we chose the one to be 'on' with a meaningless little jingle that went:

> "Sulta pulta poota par
> Tick you alakazar,
> Sulta pulta poota par
> Vonce."

This was said over and over again until all were eliminated except one, and he was "on".

One girl named Carrie, who lived in Clifton Terrace, introduced us to a new jingle for deciding who was 'on'. It went:

> "Queen Queen Caroline
> Dipped her nose in vaseline,
> Vaseline made it shine;
> Queen Queen Caroline."

When I was twelve or thirteen I went out night after night with the other kids to play Hide-and-Seek. I was the only one unlucky enough to be going to a grammar school, and should have been in the house doing my homework or violin practice. We played a more sophisticated form of the game, and in the ill-lit streets and terraces we climbed walls, lay on tops of them in a huddle and frightened people, traipsed over people's back-gardens, and generally made a nuisance of ourselves.

Like skipping, hop-scotch was a girl's game. It was always played on the blue bricks of the pavement, in beds that were elaborately drawn with chalk filched from the classroom by one of the older girls.

On our way home from school we played rolling marbles in the gutter. 'Marlies', we called them, and 'glarnies' if they were made of glass. I have broken many a glass pop bottle to get the 'glarny' out.

Some of our games were very energetic, even vicious. There was Hopping Ginny which meant 'bunting' others as they hopped across the road, and trying to knock them down or, at least, off balance. Then there was Warning, when half the boys formed one team and bent double to make a line with heads to bottoms and hands clutching the boy in front. After shouting "Warning!" from the other side of the road, the best jumper in the other team raced across and leap-frogged over as many backs as he could to reach the first boy in the line whose head was against the stomach of a boy standing against the wall. The rest followed, and with the last hanging on like grim death, the leader shouted:

"Two, four, six, eight, ten,
All my men
Off agen.
Warning!"

at which those on top struggled to get off while those underneath collapsed with the weight or through the violence of the running leaps. There would be a sprawling mass on the pavement, and often some surreptitious rib-jabbing as the tangle sorted itself out. Usually one or two of the smaller lads ran home crying and holding some part of their anatomy.

We played many such games in the street before the motor-car and lorry took over. We made long slides when snow had fallen, and hardly noticed the bitter weather. We cried: "Whip, whip behind the cart!" when a boy — whom we knew we could lick in a fight — was seen running and hanging on behind a trotting horse and cart. When the driver turned and took a cut with his whip, even though he could not see the culprit, we were greatly amused; more so, if the whip found its target and sent the boy scurrying to the pavement with a weal across his face.

There was a period, after the end of the Great War, when our usual Nov. 5th thunderflashes gave way to cannon. These fireworks were shorter but much fatter, and exploded with a tremendous bang. In our building we discovered that by putting them under a dust-bin lid, the lid was lifted five or six feet off the ground when the firework went off.

We took our discovery to one of the terraces across the road, and the kids there were delighted. Unfortunately when we were demonstrating, a boy strayed in the way and the galvanised lid came down on his head. It might have brained him; instead he set up a howl and his mother came rushing out. We fled in all directions.

The boy's head must have bled considerably, because he was taken to the hospital and had several stitches. But he was out in the back yard a day or two later, grinning away and quite pleased because his bandaged head made him the object of attention.

After that we used no more dust-bin lids but buried cannons in the garden, surrounded them with soil and small stones so just the blue paper showed, lit it, and scampered off to the nearest shed. A second or two after the explosion, earth and stones rattled down on the corrugated roof. It was like being in a dugout during the war. We were all children of men who had fought and lived to tell.

Talking of Bonfire Night, I recall a time when fire-cans were popular. We made holes in old treacle tins and put long handles of wire on them. After getting hot cinders from the fireplace we sallied forth swinging them furiously. I often think our parents must have been extremely patient and co-operative, or else would do anything to be rid off us while they did the housework or the washing or cooked dinner.

The fire-cans were easily kept alight; we scavenged local dust-bins for cinders and went round the streets, swinging our cans, in search of bits of coal near cellars where the coalman had delivered coal and the pavement was yet to be swept.

And woe betide anyone who came too near while we swung our fire-cans; if we happened to hit anything the live coals shot out in all directions.

Some of our activities seemed seasonal, like whip-and-top, pea-shooters, potato-guns, and catapults; perhaps they were dictated by the new stocks delivered to toy shops.

Hoop-la was definitely a summer game, for it meant sitting on the pavement — much cleaner, incidentally, than they are now, because housewives swept or washed them every day, and there were not nearly so many dogs to foul them. Items like discarded and broken ornaments, brooches with stones missing, and battered toys, were set out, and by paying a cigarette card another child could have a wire ring and try to get it over something he wanted.

Cigarette cards were our currency. During the Great War my father enclosed cigarette cards for me in his letters home. I think most of the kids had a similar source of supply.

We played games with them, of course, like 'skims-on' and 'skims-the-far'est'. The actual pictures meant very little to us, and the cards became dog-eared and dirty, but they were still cigarette cards!

In the safety of the green patches hidden among high-rise flats, perhaps Birmingham children still play the same games. I only know what we did in those far-off days when life had something that now seems lost. But perhaps that is how things always look to an ageing generation.

## 13

## CYCLING DAYS

In 'The Birmingham I Remember' I told of my first bicycle, a James Roadster, which my parents bought from Wintle's shop on the corner of Highgate Road and Woodfield Road when I started at Yardley Grammar School, and also of my second bicycle from Joe Cooke's on Stratford Road in 1927. This was an Imperial Petrel racer with celluloid mudguards, rat-trap pedals, and a fixed wheel. I became a member of the Cyclists' Touring Club, and clubmen disdained free wheels. I wonder why! It was so silly.

There was one drawback: almost daily I rode over the uneven teak blocks of Stratford Road, and often had to negotiate the tramlines there and in Warwick Road. In bad weather the very narrow tyres had a nasty habit of skidding, and I landed on my back in the muddy road more often than I care to remember.

During the next three or four years I saw much of the surrounding countryside. I bought 'Cycling' every Friday, read 'Wayfarer' with great avidity, and admired the sketches of a man named Paterson (I wish I could have got an original). I kept a chart of my mileage (a cyclometer on the front wheel was a must) and did the '100-in-8' quite comfortably on at least two occasions.

Our favourite place was Malvern, but the road out of Birmingham we liked best was the one to Hagley, which we joined at Five Ways. I still recall with pleasure the times we rode through Bewdley, Cleobury Mortimer, over the Clee Hills and down into Ludlow. After a day beside the River Teme we would ride back through Tenbury Wells to Holt Fleet where, along with dozens of other cyclists, we washed under the pump and had tea, first in the cottage, and a year or so later, when the family could afford it, in a long wooden hut they had built. And tea consisted of a boiled egg or peaches and cream, jam, as much bread-and-butter as we could eat and as much tea as we could drink — and the cost was one and sixpence. There was a man and his wife — a very friendly couple who looked as if they had just stepped out of Dickens — and his mother, an old but sprightly lady who ran around handing out plates of bread-and-butter. She was full of laughter and always wore a long white pinafore, stiffly starched, and a flowered sun-bonnet.

Stratford-upon-Avon was almost on our doorstep, and we did not consider our ride had really begun until we had crossed the bridge over the Avon. A small group of us rode together; we were all members of the C.T.C. but had formed a cycling club of our own and called it EMAS DINO. It sounded like a Latin tag, but stood for 'Every mile a smile — distance is no object'. I was the club's secretary and still have my badge, but the ingenious name was the brain-child of Frank Hubball.

On one occasion — a Sunday morning, of course — when the air was very cold and frosty and full of sparkling sunshine, we were cycling through Lapworth when we saw that the canal was frozen over and some children were on the ice. It was more than we could resist: we took our bikes on to the frozen canal and cycled, occasionally one of us skidding and coming a cropper mid laughter from the rest, to the Happy Valley.

The Happy Valley! It was on the canal somewhere beyond Yardley Wood Road where thousands of council houses were to be built in the 1930s. Before that the area was silvan countryside, and there were pleasure gardens, swings, picnic spots, tearooms where mineral waters and jugs of tea could be obtained, and boats for hire.

In the twenties and thirties, and for many years before that, I am told, cycling was a way of life for thousands of people. It was, in fact, the era of the push-bike — though we, the elite, objected to the term PUSH-bike. We greeted other wheelmen we encountered as we rode, with "Cheerio!" and went for miles on byroads without seeing a motorcar. The black-and-gold C.T.C. sign was prominent in almost every village, and at weekends and bank holidays hundreds of cyclists with dropped handlebars could be seen at such places as Matlock, Dovedale, Alton Towers, and Symonds Yat.

On my Imperial Petrel I toured North Wales, the Peak District, and Devon, apart from halcyon days and week-ends in Charnwood Forest, the Cotswolds, Cannock Chase, the Edge Hills and every part of Warwickshire, Worcestershire, Gloucestershire, and glorious Shropshire. I knew their by-ways and field paths and wherever light-weight bicycles could be ridden, pushed, or carried.

I bought a map showing the counties of Britain and shaded in each county as I visited it. It became something of a fetish. In 1928 I cycled alone to the West Country taking in as many counties as I could, and went just inside remote Cornwall, to Bude, in order to be able to include that Delectable Duchy.

Although I have been into a great many countries since, that cycle tour in 1928, when I was 17, stands out in my mind. I felt lonely and homesick even as I cycled along Pebble Mill Road to Bristol Road. On that first day I climbed the rock at Symonds Yat, diverted from my route in order to look at Goodrich Castle, and stayed the night at Monmouth where Henry V was born, or "porn" as Fluellen would have said.

The following day I travelled along that glorious road beside the River Wye, past Tintern Abbey, to Cardiff and stayed at another house whose address was in my C.T.C. handbook. Next morning I rode over the cobbles of Bute Street to where I boarded a paddle-steamer, and was sick all the way to Lynmouth. Four or five people were landed in the small boat which rowed out to take us off the steamer by way of one of the paddles, and I staggered up the wet causeway with my bicycle feeling very sorry for myself.

I thought Lynmouth was the most wonderful place on earth. I walked along North Walk to the Valley of Rocks without seeing anything living but seabirds and wild horses, and as I had recently read enchanting 'Lorna Doone' I visualised John Ridd, blazing with temper, standing on a high rocky ledge and hurling a goat into the sea far below.

Three incidents stand out in my mind about Bideford. In the main street a group of Welsh miners were singing for coppers; at the end of the quay that Amyas Leigh strolled along in the days of Good Queen Bess, was a tall white statue of Charles Kingsley, the man who had written 'Westward-Ho!'; and the elderly couple at whose cottage I stayed, and whose address was in the C.T.C. handbook, charged me only three and ninepence for cocoa, bread and cheese and pickled onions, bed for the night, and a hearty breakfast next morning. That was cheap, even for 1928.

Unfortunately our cycling days lasted only a few years. One of our little group had a motor-cycle, and that started the rot. Within a year we all had motor-bikes, and our conversation centred round magnetoes, plugs, and speed. Mine was a fairly new James two-stroke, and I was proud of the fact that instead of a wedge petrol tank, it had a saddle-tank, which was considered very up-to-date!

## 14

## HANDSWORTH

Mary and I often visited a couple living on the first floor of one of those large houses just past Sandwell Road in Holyhead Road, so by the time we moved into a flat in Clarence Road, almost opposite, we were familiar with the bus route from Snow Hill station to Station Road.

The buses were 72, 74, and 75. The 72 was a Birmingham Corporation bus and turned back at the West Bromwich boundary. The 74 and 75, also starting from Snow Hill Station, had blue upper decks and went to Dudley and Wednesbury. After crossing the City boundary the conductor issued new tickets and collected more fares.

It was interesting to note the difference in the voices of people going beyond the boundary. Possibly it is as apparent today as it was forty years ago. A Brummie recognises a Black Country person by his speech. There is a difference, though actors in Birmingham roles on T.V. invariably imitate Black Country folk.

We moved into the Handsworth flat a few months before I went into the army, but up to then Handsworth could have changed very little in my lifetime. It has now, from what I hear, and I am merely stating a fact when I say I wouldn't live there now at any price!

Although our address was 5, Clarence Road, the flat looked out on to Holyhead Road. We were still there when our daughter was born in 1952, and I mention it to demonstrate how life has changed. After going with Mary in an ambulance to Dudley Road Hospital late one night, I walked home between 2 and 4 in the morning through Winson Green, past the prison, and up Boulton Road to Soho Road. I have been told that to do it now would be more than my life was worth.

Our flat was over a large Corporation Electricity Supply Department showroom; next door was a Co-op, and then Woodland Road where a public air-raid shelter was built. It held a great many people and had a chemical toilet at the far end that was used far more than it should have been. I spent many nights in there with Mary before I went away, and she spent many more before the war was over.

After Woodland Road came Station Road, Crocketts Road, and a long line of houses with small front gardens, to Booth Street and the Regent Cinema.

On the opposite side of Holyhead Road were the big houses I have mentioned, including Dr. Thompson's, until the front gardens ended abruptly for the Albion, a pleasant little cinema. We often went there. On the other side of Sandwell Road was the New Inns.

I attended a meeting there in 1946 to enrol in the British Legion. The meeting was held in a big room full of ex-servicemen. As names were called candidates stood up and answered questions. When I said that my rank on leaving the army was Warrant Officer, a good-natured booing broke out, with hissing and catcalls.

Below the Regent Cinema, Soho Road, a continuation of Holyhead Road, was all shops on both sides. No need to go to Town if you lived in Handsworth: in Soho Road you could get everything you needed, and possibly cheaper than in Corporation or New Street. There was a railway station, too, and another cinema that must have been built when cinemas were called picture-houses.

On the left at the bottom of the hill — for it was a long, steady descent from our flat — was a large sombre building behind iron railings set on a brick wall and with an ugly clock tower. It was the public library and was once the Council House. Handsworth had been a separate borough until it was absorbed by the great Midland metropolis.

I went regularly to Handsworth library. It was very good. Somewhere near, perhaps I saw it on a lamp-post, was the double knot of Staffordshire, a symbol that figured prominently in the county's coat-of-arms. It represented, so I was told, the custom of local magistrates to have miscreants hanged in pairs in order to economise on rope.

Continuing towards Town, the road descended more rapidly to Hockley Brook where there was a bus shelter in the middle of the road and a cinema on the left-hand side. Hockley Brook was always a difficult crossing, and a policeman was usually on point duty. I say "difficult" because traffic was already heavy when we went to Handsworth.

The bus then passed through the famous — or notorious — jewellery quarter where the main road was now called Great Hampton Street. Many of the back street houses were sweat shops whose rooms were occupied by rows of girls on piece work making cheap costume jewellery. In dusty little rooms upstairs one or two craftsmen produced beautiful rings, brooches, pendants, and bracelets with costly gems exquisitely set in gold and platinum. I visited such a place in 1936 to buy Mary's engagement ring — through a friend, of course!

The bus into Town crossed over to Livery Street and ran beside innumerable railway arches containing warehouses, to the terminus in Colmore Row. For the journey out of Town, the bus went down Snow Hill with the other end of the arches on the left again, to join Great Hampton Street.

The mention of Livery Street reminds me that when any of us sulked my father would say: "You've got a face as long as Livery Street." And if we spoke out of turn he would tell us that our tongues were as long as Livery Street. I used to think that this was an expression of his own, but I have since learned that it was based on an old Brummagem saying. Livery Street, it seems, was once the longest street in Town and that it was always drearily monotonous.

We seldom walked along Clarence Road. Like other roads on our side of Holyhead Road it went down to Smethwick, and our inclination rarely took us in that direction. We thought of it as a region of factories and smoke and 'dark satanic mills'.

In the introduction to 'The Birmingham I Remember' I said we never got to know a district as intimately as we knew the one of our childhood. When I think of the fourteen adult years spent in Handsworth I realise the truth of this, and of the great difference between the mind of an adult and the unconscious searching and uncomplicated mind of a child.

My recollection of Handsworth is not nearly as sharply defined as that of Sparkbrook, Sparkhill, and Balsall Heath. And no matter where I have lived since my childhood, there has been something lacking, something intangible and elusive.

There is, I feel, a sharp dividing line somewhere in life, and that those early years were possessed of a kind of romantic unreality. Or was theirs the Reality? Perhaps Wordsworth was as near to it as man can be when he wrote:

There was a time when meadow, grove, and stream,
The earth, and every common sight,
To me did seem
Apparell'd in celestial light,
The glory and the freshness of a dream.
It is not now as it has been of yore;—
Turn wheresoe'er I may
By night or day,
The things which I have seen I now can see no more...

## 15

## YARDLEY GRAMMAR SCHOOL

Some years ago my sister-on-law, Grace Barton, now Wilkins, read in a newspaper that Mr. Edgerton, headmaster of a Birmingham primary school, was to retire. She remembered him when he taught at Dennis Road School. I, too, remembered him when, as a student, he came to Stratford Road School for a few weeks.

I wrote telling him this and wishing him a happy retirement. When he replied he enclosed a faded photograph of the class in 1920. Mr. Irwin was standing at the back of the classroom, and Mr. Edgerton, looking very young, was beside the window into the hall. I was sitting up straight, my arms folded, and wearing the grey Norfolk jacket I clearly remembered.

There were sixty boys in the class; they all looked incredibly familiar, and after a lapse of more than 60 years I could name every one of them. Three of the boys wore caps, and I was reminded that boys with ringworm had their heads completely shaved and were allowed to wear caps in class until their hair grew again. Mary has told me that girls with the same infection wore little woollen hats.

Memory plays strange tricks. Although I could name all the boys in that class, today I often cannot put names to people I know well and whom I see every day. And I can never remember the number of my car.

A nephew had told me that my age is responsible, but I replied that it was because I was now more selective in what I committed to memory, and that I subconsciously rejected the unimportant. He laughed and said I couldn't face facts. Sorrowfully I have to admit that he was right.

I started at Yardley Grammar School in 1923 and can remember the names of the children in 2A that year with Miss Lloyd as our form mistress. One of the few disappointments I have had with the publication of 'The Birmingham I Remember' is that while many Sparkbrook people who knew me at Stratford Road School have written to me, only one in my form at Yardley has done so. That was Edith Abel whom I mentioned in the introduction.

I remember having my desk next to Edith's in the Art Room. It was large and airy, and the Art Master was a man named Thomas. We were all rather scared of his violent temper (probably simulated), fiery tongue, and habit of walking round with a ruler or set square and lashing out left and right at girls as well as boys.

On this particular occasion he had told us to draw a large shield on our paper then design a suitable escutcheon depicting our name. Edith drew and painted a bell, and told me that it represented Abel. After some thought I drew and painted a sprig of hawthorn in bloom — or what was supposed to represent hawthorn — and two crossed tridents superimposed on the letter H. Beneath these were leaping flames.

Mr. Thomas passed round the class looking at what we had done, occasionally shouting at some poor wretch and hitting him across the back of the neck with his ruler.

He stood behind me and I held my breath.

"What's this supposed to mean?" he demanded.

Sheepishly I told him that the flowers represented "may", that the flames meant "hell", and that the two tridents crossed out the aitch.

After looking at it for a few moments he said in a normal voice: "Is this your idea of a joke, boy?"

I vigorously denied that it wasn't — which was true — and he walked away.

A few weeks later I had a new black tin of Reeve's water colours. Mr. Thomas saw them and asked if I'd put my name on the box.

I said: "No, sir. Not yet," and expected a whack on the side of the head.

Instead he said: "Come along and I'll put it on for you."

He sat down at his desk and picked up a pair of dividers.

"What's your first name?" he asked.

"Leslie, sir," I replied.

Beautifully he scratched 'Lesley Mayell' on the back of the box.

I did not dare tell him that I spelt my name 'Leslie', but I felt slightly superior: I knew, but he did not, that 'Lesley' was a girl's name.

A few years ago Mary and I paid a visit to our old school. From Warwick Road it looked much the same as it had always looked, but it spewed temporary classrooms all over the boys' playground in Medina Road and the girls' in Reddings Lane. School had just finished and a noisy multiracial multitude was emerging. The headmaster, looking out-of-place in Mr. Lunn's sanctum sanctorum, gave us permission to look around the school. We did so, but neither of us could identify it with the quiet, cultured institution we had once known. Youths still rampaged around, and the atmosphere was all wrong.

There had been structural alterations, of course, but the hall was much the same, though it looked smaller and somehow had lost the dignity it once

51

had. At the far corner of the balcony was the room used by 2A in 1923, but I was quite unmoved. This was a comprehensive school now, and a school, like a church, is not merely the building.

Since our visit to Yardley School — that is its nomenclature now — I have acquired a book about Yardley Grammar School and the traditions it had achieved since it was erected early in the century. Entitled 'Fifty Years of Yardley — 1904 to 1954', it contains a list of the men and women who taught there. Some had already died when the book was published. I remember little Miss Haworth with her eye-glasses and her catarrh who was killed in a road accident in France in 1926. A stained glass window was dedicated to her memory in the new library.

Mr. Marsh, big and full of fun and mathematics, died while still at Yardley in 1940; and Miss Waite who, in my memory, will always be the tall, brownhaired lady who taught us French, died in 1945. Henry Pontefract Lunn, the headmaster, reached retirement in 1940 and died 6 years later.

At the outbreak of war I was sent there to distribute gas-masks to people living in the area. There were three sizes — small, medium, and large — and I sat at a table with the cardboard boxes beside me.

I recall the different reactions of the women as they tried on the respirators — they were mostly women at that time of the day. Some treated the whole thing as a joke, and laughed when they saw their friends in masks and the noise made by the rubber when they breathed out. Perhaps they could not adjust their minds to the reality of war. Others looked rather scared but smiled with bravado. Many old women simply panicked; one, full of self-pity, cried and said: "I never thought I'd live to see the day when I had to wear one of these."

I saw some of the teachers I had known — masters and mistresses, we had called them — including Mr. Lunn and Miss Rattray, the senior mistress. Classes were taking place, and Miss Rattray said people should not try their respirators on when the children were around for fear of frightening them.

A police inspector heard her and said in a loud voice: "Madam. The sooner children see them being worn and get used to them, the better."

I agreed with him. We were not to know that Hitler would not use gas. The only reason the Fuhrer of the Third Reich refrained was because he knew that this time it would not take us by surprise, and that German armies and cities would in turn be drenched with gas. It was certainly not humanitarianism that stopped the Germans — there was no humanitarianism there — but the fear of reprisal. The present-day anti-nuclear organisations have still to learn the lesson of safety through a deterrent.

18. *The Happy Valley*

*19a.  Birmingham Cyclists, 1929/30*
*Harry Nicholls*

*19b.  Tandem riders, about 1930*
*W. Broughton*

20.   *The King and Queen in Calthorpe Park, 1939*

21.  *Handsworth Library*

But I must not allow personal views to intrude. This is a book about Birmingham, not about mankind and poison gas 'after two thousand years of Mass'.

I will conclude this chapter about Yardley Grammar School — whose story could be that of any Birmingham grammar school — by telling how I wandered round my old school during the lunch period that day, and came across Mr. Hudson, the woodwork master, in his workshop. I made myself known to him.

He talked as he used to talk to us in class. It was amusing to listen to this elderly man and realise that he had never grown up. Apparently he had spent the vacation in the Lake District, and spoke of the climbing he had done. He had scaled the highest and most dangerous peaks without the slightest fear.

"I was like that when I played cricket," he said, and I thought to myself: "Here it comes!"

It was a joke among the boys years ago that no matter what Soapy began talking about, he always ended up talking about cricket. He went on to tell me that he would face the fastest bowler with equanimity, and when fielding would get as close as he could to the batsman.

Soapy Hudson remained at Yardley Grammar School until he retired in 1945; he died in 1952. R.I.P.

# 16

## WIRELESS

My introduction to radio was rather vague. A pole was erected in the garden of a house 'over the boards', which was how we referred to the houses in Tillingham Street whose gardens backed on to ours in Turner Street. We knew who had put the pole there: it was Bernie's older brother. Bernie was our age, and his mother was a thin little red-faced woman who never smiled and who shouted "Bernie!" several times a day in a raucous voice that could be heard in at least three buildings in Turner Street as well as 'over the boards'.

But to get back to wireless. Bernie's brother must have been something of a local radio pioneer for we had no idea why the pole was there until my sister Doris, who must have been talking to Bernie's big brother, told us that something on the top of the pole gathered in the sound.

Perhaps it was in 1920 or 1921 that poles began to appear in gardens all over the neighbourhood. They carried a wire that ran the length of the garden and back yard to a hook in the bedroom window frame, then down through a hole into the living room to the crystal set. Our set was made by Bob Eastwood who was courting cousin Olive. It was just a small piece of wood with two little coils of wire, one of which moved, four terminals, and a tiny piece of thin twisted wire, the cat's-whisker, that touched a crystal fixed in a little brass cup. Earphones went to two of the terminals, a wire from the aerial to another, and the earth wire to the fourth. It was the earth wire that gave the most trouble. It was wound round the tap in the back kitchen and brought under the door to the set.

I think wireless was the first nail in the coffin of family music. For as long as could be remembered, folk had gathered round the ubiquitous piano to sing, but now the person who was listening in, usually the dad, would say: "Shush!" to anyone who spoke as he fiddled about with the cat's-whisker to find "a good spot" on the crystal.

When the backdoor was opened there was an immediate concerted cry of: "Mind the wire!" I remember an occasion when someone entering caught the door against the wire and brought the whole apparatus down in chaos, pulling the earphones off my father's head.

I cannot say that I was an enthusiastic listener in those early days — I suppose I was always off playing in the street or Sparkhill Park — but Jack Eastwood and I joined 5IT, wore our badges, and on Saturday afternoons went to a tiny studio in New Street to hear our radio aunties and uncles talk about the mysteries of wireless.

What went on in our house concerning the radio took place in every home in our building, in most of the homes in Sparkbrook, and indeed throughout the City.

Later we had a valve set and Bob put it into a box-like cabinet that stood on a small bamboo table. He was a pattern maker at the Wolseley Works in Saltley before moving to the Rolls Royce, Derby.

There were five large valves in the cabinet, and a box for the high tension which consisted of about 24 flash-lamp batteries connected in series. On the floor was a stout wooden box painted black with our name in white. It contained the accumulator. The box had a thick strap nailed to it because the accumulator had to be carried to a shop to be re-charged fairly often. Inside the cabinet was another battery that had two or three little plugs, called wander plugs, inserted into it.

On top of the cabinet was a large, brown, trumpet-like loud speaker, but quietness was still demanded by the person tuning in. I knew many who sat all evening twiddling little knobs. London (2LO) could now be heard, and occasionally the twiddler announced excitedly that he had "got a foreigner".

## 17

# HOMES

Although I was born in Stratford Road I have little recollection of it. It was at 75, Turner Street, a short distance away, that I grew from babyhood into childhood and from childhood into manhood. The house was typical of those built in Sparkbrook, in other suburbs of Birmingham, and, I suppose, in most towns during the latter part of Queen Victoria's reign. The only difference was that some houses had tiny front gardens, others had a passage that ran from the front door to the living room, and others opened from the front room directly on to the street. Ours was like that.

At night our front room was in darkness unless the gas was lit for someone who called to see my mother about business. In 1933 we had electricity installed, and soon afterwards a gas-fire replaced the open grate. The room, sometimes called the parlour, had an atmosphere of its own. It was the "best" room, over-furnished and used only on Christmas Day and on a Sunday when we had a party, but parties virtually ceased when Olive and Doris married and left home.

Family photographs abounded: they were on the walls, the mantel shelf, and the sideboard. And the sideboard had numerous little shelves, several mirrors, and a massive multi-vase piece with long glass trumpets, sticks of twisted coloured glass, and little glass hanging baskets. A cut-glass and EPNS cruet with an ebony handle, a crock biscuit barrel, and a number of small ornaments were also on the sideboard.

On the mantel piece, besides framed photographs, were two large vases and a matching crock clock that never went in my time, and scattered about the room, wherever space could be found, were pieces of coat-of-arms china that Olive, and later Doris, had brought back from holidays. I think everyone bought them when they went to the seaside; they were about one shilling (1/-) each. I don't know what happened to them; they were probably thrown away like so many other things. We had a brass fender with matching fire-irons once, but I don't know what happened to those, either, and I certainly didn't care at the time.

A pink flower-pot containing an aspidistra stood on a tripod of thick bamboo staves in the window. Many years later I took the tripod to pieces and used the bamboos as the staffs of Babylonian soldiers in a play based on Psalm 137, 'By the rivers of Babylon...'

Between the parlour and the living room were the stairs.

In the middle of the living room was a deal table (later replaced by a stained extending one) that my mother scrubbed white every Saturday morning before going shopping up 'the Lane'. I remember having breakfast as I watched her scrub the red quarries and blacklead the grate.

On each side of the fire-place was a wooden armchair; two upholstered dining room chairs were pushed under the table. There was not much room to pass between the piano and the table because of the piano stool, but this served as a seat when we were all in to a meal.

Against the wall, and between the door to the stairs and the one to the pantry, was a sofa — we called it the couch — and opposite was the window, against which was a treadle sewing machine, and the door to the back kitchen.

The fire-place was the focal point. It had a steel guard made by my grandfather Yardley; it had three round bars which my mother kept bright with emery paper; on the top bar were little brass rings to spin and amuse the children. My mother, who was a small woman, stood on the bottom bar to reach the mantel shelf where there was always a collection of ornaments, brass candlesticks, letters, a perpetual calendar, and I don't know what. A tasselled green runner was tacked to the wooden mantelpiece, and a brass chain was slung across for airing small garments.

The fire-place, or grate, was a masterpiece of the ironfounders' craft. It had elaborate panels, hobs, and on the right-hand side an oven with a brass knob. On the hot hob, the one over the oven, was an iron kettle with a thick brass handle that had a core of steel running through it, and a brass knob on the iron lid. Two marbles rolled about inside: my grandmother told me they were to keep the bottom of the kettle clean. It always contained hot water which could be quickly brought to the boil by hanging the kettle from a wide, iron swivel hook on a rod that went into the grate over the fire.

In winter I had the oven plate wrapped in newspaper at night to warm my feet in bed, and Olive and Doris had a brick that was put into the oven after tea. It was a bone of contention between the girls and me, because the brick retained the heat longer. Next morning the oven plate was like ice, but the brick was still warm.

Below the fire was a dust preventer: it stopped the ashes falling on the thick rug my grandmother had made out of bits of cloth backed by hessian. The dust preventer was made of cast iron and was very heavy; on the front was the face of Livingstone. My mother blackleaded and polished it every Saturday morning. It probably finished up like the grate — smashed by a sledge hammer — when my mother had a modern fire-place installed.

In the back kitchen were a mangle, a black iron gas stove, the sink, and the copper. On washing-days the furnace beneath the copper was fed with wet slack. Above the copper were some shelves and beside it an old chair, on which my grandmother sat when she had withdrawn from the living room because she was not on speaking terms with my parents. Her glass and bottle of stout would be on the copper-lid.

Before she turned 'funny' I would fetch her bottle of Mitchells and Butlers Nourishing Stout from Preston's out-door. It cost seven pence. In cold weather she would put sugar into the glass and the end of the poker made red-hot by being stuck between the bars of the grate. The stout would hiss and steam, and make a lot of brown froth. Quick as lightning I would take a sip as soon as her back was turned.

Talking of going to Preston's, I used to fetch my father half-a-pint of ale on Sunday mornings after he returned from the Great War. I had to take a bottle and the ale was drawn into a measure from taps beneath decorated crock pump handles. It was then poured into the bottle through a copper tun dish. When the cork had been replaced it was covered with a label. The half-pint of draught ale cost two pence.

The back kitchen was unplastered; the bricks were colour-washed pink. It was unlighted until we had an electric point put in in 1933. Over it was the little bedroom where I slept until Doris married in 1932. It never did have a light, and when I went to bed I took a lighted candle. During the day I frequently went up to that room for the fun of climbing through the window out on to the roof of the W.C., from there on to the corrugated iron roof of the shed, and thence to the back yard by sliding down a judiciously placed long clothes prop.

With the exception of the back kitchen and the little bedrom, the rooms were gas-lit: four lights in all. I remember when we changed from an upright mantle in the living room to an inverted one. My mother bought the fittings from a shop just past Highgate Road in Ladypool Road. Those upright mantles were hung on a delicate crutch of white pipeclay. I wonder if they are still made! We had to fire a new mantle. After it had flared up for a moment, we could use it, but it was extremely vulnerable: the least touch turned it to white dust. After changing from upright to inverted we turned on the gas by pulling a chain with a little ring on the end. Before that we used to turn a tap.

In 'The Birmingham I Remember' I mentioned a portrait of Joseph Chamberlain hanging in our living room. There were other large pictures. There was one of Norma Talmadge, a famous screen beauty of those days. It was sent to Olive by 'The Picturegoer', a popular magazine she bought each week. And there was a framed print of a boy dressed like little Lord Fauntleroy; he held a bridle behind his back as he enticed a horse with an apple while his two little sisters watched him. Other houses would have "Highland Cattle" or "Monarch of the Glen" on their walls.

I have mentioned the pantry. Ours opened out of the living room and had many shelves. We often heard or saw a mouse scampering along one of them;

when we did my mother put a bit of cheese on a mouse-trap and usually caught the culprit. Her usual comment was "I'll have to get some adamant to fill up the holes !" But I don't think she ever did.

It was through the pantry that we went down into the cellar, where the coal was kept. It came down through a hole covered by a grating in the street. My mother took the heavy chain off the grating when the coalman was due, and when she heard it raised listened at the top of the cellar steps and counted the number of sacks he put down to make sure she was not overcharged.

Coalmen drove their horses slowly round the streets, and shouted: "Coal! Coal!" The price was one and tenpence a hundredweight (1/10d). Their flat carts not only carried bags of coal but a large pair of scales. I understand they were obliged to have those by the law.

The penny-in-the-slot gasmeter was fixed in the cellar where the pipe came in from the street. When "the gas was going" the light went dim; my mother would give me tuppence to put in the meter. At night I went down in pitch darkness with my hands in front of me as I crossed the cellar until my finger-tips told me that I had reached the meter. On Saturday nights I had to walk with special care because the Sunday joint of beef, mutton, or pork hung from a rafter by a hook. It was the coolest place in the house.

The rafters were very low and the time came when I felt them touch my head. Soon I was bending, like the other members of the family, when I went down to fetch a bucket of coal or put money in the meter.

When the gasman came I watched him count the pennies in twelves on the table and put them into 5/- bags which he dropped into a large leather bag he carried. He then made an entry in his book and gave my mother a receipt.

I remember being taken one night into our neighbour's cellar and put into a bed down there. Their cellar was the same as ours but it had a gas jet. I was told that Zeppelins were passing over.

Each day we had several callers: baker, milkman, gypsies, pedlars; every Tuesday the insurance men came, and every Monday morning the rent-collector, whom we called the landlord. He was a big fellow who wore a trilby and a raincoat, and carried a book and an indelible pencil. He always walked straight into the house without knocking. He had an air of authority but was always jolly, called me "Curly!" and ruffled my hair. We were all tenants; buying a house through a building society was unheard of in those days as far as I knew.

And that was 75, Turner Street, Sparkbrook, when I was a child. It no longer exists. Nor, indeed, does Turner Street.

## 18

## WASHING-DAY

Tuesday was washing-day at our house. It was either Monday or Tuesday throughout our building and over the boards in Tillingham Street.

My earliest memory of washing-days is associated with the thump-thump-thump of dollies in clothes tubs far and near. It was done in back yards by women in hessian aprons with their sleeves rolled up, and is now among the lost sounds like the cries of London.

I hated washing-days — the steam and dampness, the draughty living room and the make-shift dinner. While I was going to Yardley I stayed at school for dinner on Tuesdays.

During the week the dirty clothes were put into the clothes closet, a tiny room that went off the front bedroom, and washing-day began as soon as dad, Olive, and Doris had gone off to work or school. I often helped my mother to drag the clothes round the bedroom and throw them down the stairs. As she descended she kicked those that had not gone to the bottom until they were all down. They were then taken through the living room into the back kitchen.

Here the mangle had been pulled out and a fire was already burning under the copper. When the clothes were put into the boiling soapy water, my mother continually pressed them down with a copper stick — later on she used a round ruler I had made at 'manual' after I went into the Big Boys at Stratford Road School. The soapy water soon became a dirty grey.

The washed clothes were eventually put through the large wooden rollers of the mangle. I won't attempt to describe the mangle: there was once one in every home and there are still plenty of them around. Until recently they were left outside to rust; now they have become collectors' items.

Washing-day ended at four or soon after. In winter dusk was already setting in, and it always seemed cold and dreary. My mother emptied her tub by the simple expedient of rolling it on its side, causing the warm, grey, soapy water to cover the entire back yard. This was then swept and the water brushed down the drains. There were two: one was our own that water from the sink went into; the other we shared with the people next door: it was below the boards, half in their yard and half in ours.

Seeing our yard in my mind's eye reminds me that there was virginia creeper all along the boards between us and next door, and that it climbed up the backs of the two houses. It made our living room darker than it should have been, but virginia creeper and ivy on the walls of houses were very popular in those days.

Best of all I remember the 'good' washing-days when the sun shone and the breeze made the clothes flap on the long line that stretched the length of the garden, and the sheets to billow like the sails of a galleon.

The following day, when the clothes had been ironed, they were put to air on a line stretched across the living room, and anyone coming from the front room or down the stairs had to duck under them.

## 19

## BATH NIGHT

My mother, the youngest of a large family, had a brother 20 years older than herself. Her mother, Louisa Maria Yardley, nee Thorp, was born in 1836 and never learned to read or write. She lived with us when I was a small child, and I can remember her bathing me in a small galvanised bath in front of the fire. We had two such baths, one a bit bigger than the other. They were kept in the back kitchen. When a bit older I bathed myself in the copper on washing-day in the light of a candle.

Bathrooms were unknown in Turner Street. There was one at the Ivor Billiard Hall in Showell Green Lane where my uncle, aunt, and cousins lived, but that was different: it was not an ordinary house, and I remember thinking what a waste of a room it was. The bath, originally white, had turned yellow, and was a queer shape: more like an armchair than a bath.

Later we had a long galvanised bath that I could lie full-length in. We kept it in the shed by the W.C. with my mother's wash tub and the garden spade and fork. It hung from a big nail knocked in the cement between the bricks.

Friday night was usually bath night. The bath was carried into the back kitchen, and a bucket of water heated on the gas stove. I don't think any of us had more than one bath a week, and that was far more than many had, as I discovered in the army years later when I was responsible for seeing that men did not avoid bath parade. But that's another story!

In the long galvanised bath I would lie and soak until the water began to get cold, and then I washed my hair. I think that is what most people did. And when the person using the bath finished, it was emptied with a galvanised bowl with a wooden handle that we called a ladle.

The water pipe ran from the sink tap through a hole knocked in the brick wall to the W.C. Here the pipe crossed a wall to the cistern. It was in this stretch that a burst frequently occurred during winter. When a thaw set in and water poured out like a fountain, we used the simple expedient of 'knocking up' the pipe with a hammer so that the W.C. could be used. The 'landlord' was notified the next time he called and then it was out of the tenant's hands. The plumber might come within a week or in a month's time.

How uncomplicated life seemed in those days!

## 20

## CONCLUSION

This really is the last time I shall use the word·'conclusion' in a collection of memories up to 1939. The reason is simple: there is nothing further for me to say.

I am very grateful to the many people who, after reading my previous book, have written to tell me what I might have said. Many of these omissions have been woven into this book, but I have to repeat that a writer must always be selective.

In writing these Further Memories of Birmingham, I have been aware that I, as a person, have intruded more than I did in the earlier book. This has been unavoidable. As I have grown older incidents have become more personalised, and other personalities more dominant. But it has always been my aim to present the Birmingham I knew before it was changed by the Luftwaffe and the bulldozers of the town planners. For me the result of my work is fairly satisfactory and comprehensive, but I know from my correspondence that there are others whose knowledge of the City of forty, fifty and sixty years ago is more extensive than my own.